THE GROWTH MINDSET CODE:
Cracking the Secrets to Success

Comprehensive Guide to Breaking Limits With a Growth Mindset, Cultivating Unlimited Possibilities

Chrío Zoë

Acknowledgement

<hr>

Writing this book has been a labor and a journey that I couldn't have undertaken without the incredible support and encouragement of many individuals. I am profoundly grateful to all those who have played a part in bringing this project to fruition.

I would like to thank each person who was instrumental in shaping my path to writing this manuscript. My sincerest appreciation goes to the countless friends and family who graciously gave me space and time to make this book become a reality.

First and foremost, I want to express my deepest gratitude to my family whose unwavering belief in me and constant encouragement have been my driving force. Your love and support have sustained me through the challenges of this creative process. I give honor to my late parents, Stephen and Pearl, whose unwavering belief has been the catalyst to propel me in this journey. Their constant encouragement and unconditional love have been my strength to pursue this endeavor. I say thank you to my siblings Michael, Anthony, Pauline and Sharon who have now passed on but are the silent voices that ignited me to write this book. Through their life, in their own small contributing way, I have come to realize that this journey we call life is valuable and how we start the journey does not dictate how we finish it.

I would like to thank all of my mentors and teachers who helped me by sharing their invaluable knowledge base with me, as they guided me from a place of knowing in shaping my ideas and refining my writing. I cherish your warm guidance, encouragement, and belief in me, and my potential and I can attest to the fact that it has been transformative. I am sincerely hoping that this book will serve as a helpful resource and companion guide on my readers' journey toward self-improvement, empowerment, and fulfillment.

I'd also like to thank the team at AIA and Publishing Services for their dedication and hard work in bringing this book to life. Your expertise coaching and guidance in outlining, design, formatting, and marketing have been pivotal in turning my manuscript into a polished publication.

Additionally, I am grateful to my dear friends, who provided much-needed moral support and encouragement during the writing process. I am forever grateful for your influence and for your push to encourage me into what you believe I could be. Thank you all for the guidance and the wisdom you shared with me as I stumbled along my sometimes-rocky road of personal growth and self-discovery. I extend my heartfelt appreciation to my friends and colleagues who provided valuable feedback, engaged in insightful discussions, and cheered me on during moments of doubt. Your enthusiasm has been contagious and uplifting.

Finally, I want to acknowledge my readers—those who will engage with this book. Your curiosity and interest in my ideas fuel my passion for writing, and I hope this book resonates with you in meaningful ways. In writing this book, I've come to realize that the journey is made sweeter by the presence of supportive souls. To all those I've mentioned and to anyone whose name might have been inadvertently omitted, please know that your impact has been immeasurable.

To all of you, your enthusiasm, engagement, and support to me have been more than appreciated. Let me end by saying once again to my readers that I applaud you for buying this book to enhance and empower your personal development. I trust that this book will meet your desire.

With heartfelt thanks,

Chrío Zoë

Contents

Introduction

Living your life feeling like you are constantly hitting an invisible yet very real ceiling can be utterly exhausting. Have you ever felt trapped by your own mind? Deep down, you know that you deserve more and can certainly achieve more, but fear always gets the better of you. The fear of the unknown, the fear of leaving your comfort zone, the failure of fear, and, surprisingly, the fear of success can paralyze you from moving forward.

As the years elapse, you realize that even you are fed up with playing small. You notice how being mediocre is no longer serving you at all. Even the prospect of going on social media might evoke unpleasant feelings in you as you watch how people are making the most of their lives and trying new things while you remain stuck in your old ways. If you've ever felt suffocated and held back from unlocking greater versions of yourself by the way you think, then you're certainly not alone. The great news is that instead of throwing the towel, you decided to face your fears and overcome them. *How do I know that?* The fact that you are reading this book on how to master having a growth mindset and escape a fixed mindset is enough evidence. Your tenacity and unwavering faith have moved you to this point. Now let's make every step of this journey of unleashing your limitless success worthwhile!

What exactly is a growth or fixed mindset? Simply put, a growth mindset is having the belief and way of thinking that your talents, skills, knowledge, qualities, and abilities can be learned and improved by putting in the relevant effort. On the other hand, having a fixed mindset means that you believe that all your skills, gifts, understanding, and abilities are innate. So you end up not seeing any room for growth. Instead, you believe that life will always be the same for you. It is this belief that demotivates people with a fixed mindset from being open to constructive feedback or trying new things. Conversely, people with a growth mindset are always open to learning and motivated to overcome their current limitations and fears because they believe that things can change.

Life is vast and packed with limitless opportunities for you to harness. However, when you are always locked in the reality of your everyday life—seeing the same people and doing the same things—and your knowledge is limited to what you already know, your perspective can easily become narrow-minded. It's only when you allow yourself to step outside what's familiar to you that many of the myriad opportunities you never thought would be available to you start to become visible in your eyes.

Life in the realm of having a fixed mindset is undoubtedly very predictable, comforting to some degree, and even enjoyable to some extent. However, it gets boring with time since repetition is the norm in that world. Doing the same things over and over again is good sometimes, but when it comes to areas like your personal growth and career advancement, it can cause you to fall drastically behind. While others learn new things and become more skilled and competent in many things, you remain with the same value and even risk having a depreciating value.

We live in a dynamic world that not only needs us to grow but also demands that we grow. Growth is what brings novelty and excitement to our lives. Think about some of the reasons why most relationships fall apart: What you may likely hear is someone complaining that they felt like they outgrew the relationship. If only one person is growing and the other stays the same without improving how they show up in the relationship, an imbalance starts to prevail. It is such dynamics that give birth to more problems that eventually make friendships, romantic relationships, and even families fall apart. What bonds people to each other is their perception of what they believe they can benefit from each other. Thus, if there is no real growth in your relationships, there can never be lasting fulfillment.

Although embracing a growth mindset would remarkably improve your relationships, it is the relationship you have with yourself that will benefit you profoundly. It's easier to love yourself when you are constantly growing and getting better in every aspect of your life. Conversely, it's way harder to foster self-love when you aren't growing. When fear is the driver instead of your faith, then that's where issues like battling with low self-esteem, low self-confidence, and low self-worth arise. Once you have a poor relationship with yourself, it becomes hard to build and maintain healthy relationships with others.

Hence, there is no doubt that the only way to unburden yourself from the horror of not ever unleashing your full potential is to discard the fixed mindset and rewire your thinking. When you embrace the growth mindset, you become unstoppable and even learn to sprint forward, even in the presence of fear and doubts.

This book is here to practically guide you on ways to alter your paradigm and adopt new ways of thinking, acting, and speaking. Your habits define you. By practicing the growth mindset, your habits will also start to transform. You will become empowered with the secrets to succeeding as you navigate living your new life with a growth mindset.

We often hear many sources encouraging us to have a growth mindset, but this can be difficult to do if you aren't sure of how exactly to do so practically. Each chapter of this book will elaborate in depth on key components you need to understand to master the growth mindset. As you read this book, I hope that you can finally say goodbye to your old life and be open to endless possibilities of success. Demand more from yourself. Now is the time to die of any old version of who you were that was keeping you stuck in unproductive habits. Remember: Everything you desire is the opposite of the reality your fears have conjured. Now it's time to get the life you were always destined for. Let's do this!

Chapter 1

What Is a Mindset?

Have you ever watched people play a sport that you enjoy very much and then heard a loud thought creep into your mind, reinforcing the idea that you can never be as good as them no matter what? It's so easy to fall into the belief that some people are just naturally good at something, while others can never master the same thing even if they try. It is such beliefs that eventually shape our minds and control the way we perceive reality.

Your mindset is what controls your choices and, ultimately, the outcome of your daily life. But what exactly is a mindset? Just as the name suggests, it is the set way in which your mind thinks and perceives reality. That way of thinking is governed by your beliefs, assumptions, and the knowledge you feed yourself and accept to be true. Your mindset then shapes your personality, which also includes your attitude towards everything. Sometimes, when life gets hard, we tend to assume that if only we had a different background, lots of wealth, or better opportunities, we would have been succeeding well. However, you can have all of that and still be unhappy and unfulfilled with your life regardless. This reveals the fact that the secret to success is not necessarily determined by the opportunities you have or don't have; instead, the condition of your mindset is what controls everything.

This is great news because it means that for you to live a successful life, you don't have to wait for opportunities that may be out of your control to have now when you think you need them. You can still be here with what you have and what you do now. The power to change your reality is already in your hands. You can unlock that power by understanding your mindset and discarding all thought patterns and beliefs that hold you back. Next, you can plant empowering beliefs and new thoughts that will help you attract the reality you wish to see. This chapter will help you unearth some of the key strategies you can put in place so that your mindset will no longer be the reason why you continue to fail in any way.

How would you describe your mindset? Have you ever wondered why you think the way you do? Or even question the core beliefs you adhere to. How exactly does the mindset form?

We come into this world as innocent babies with pretty blank slates. Then, as we grow, we start to adapt to our new world, notice many things, and pick up certain habits and mannerisms. Whatever seems to serve any need that we may have at different points in our lives is what we would then stick to and do repeatedly. For instance, if you notice that the only way your guardians or parents would give you the affection you crave is if you have serious problems, then you might develop the belief that being okay repels love from you. So you can start to always act needy by sharing about endless problems because you think that without them, you won't get the love, empathy, and attention you need. It is our mindsets that cause us to suffer or enjoy life. Therefore, it only makes sense to take an interest in understanding how your mindset has worked to your advantage up until now, conversely, making you sabotage yourself.

The mindset you have now is what you have consciously and subconsciously chosen. People are so attached to their mindsets because they believe that a set way of thinking and decoding reality prevents them from experiencing pain. Our brains are hardwired to promote survival. That is why we all have the flight and fight hormones that jump-start us into taking any necessary protective action whenever there is a perceived or real threat. This sounds good, but the problem emerges when your brain is sending the wrong information to you.

For example, not everything your mind perceives to be true is correct. Your brain can perceive that leaving your old job that makes you unhappy is not good for you because you won't ever get the security you have now. However, that's not entirely true. There are certainly many opportunities you can try out that can provide you with job security as well as meet the unmet needs you have. But the only way you would be able to have those opportunities is if you challenged your mind whenever it restrained you from doing something different, simply because anything unfamiliar to the brain sounds dangerous to it. Thus, without challenging your mindset, you can easily downplay and lock yourself in your comfort zone for years. The only way to experience what's new and potentially fulfilling is when you allow yourself to no longer be so attached to the mindset you have always had up until now.

Here is an example of how someone's mindset can cause them so much suffering unnecessarily. Paula has been feeling very sick for the last six months. She used to brush aside the pain until it became unbearably painful. She then decides to go see the doctor. When her diagnosis came, she was told that she had breast cancer. Although such news was devastating to hear, the doctor shortly after announced very positive and hopeful news. He shared that since the cancer was still in its early stages, Paula had a 94% chance of survival. If she only takes the necessary remedial actions and treatments, she will be able to bounce back to normalcy pretty soon. However, Paula didn't seem to be moved by the comforting news. She remained downcast and became very stressed. In her mind, she couldn't take in the positive feedback and believe it at all because of her beliefs. Since Paula had two close relatives who didn't survive cancer, she immediately believed that there was no chance for her to survive. This made her disregard the positive feedback and accept the false belief that she was going to die, come what may. The statistics didn't matter to her. She fell into a defeatist mindset and didn't even bother to fight for her life since she believed it was the end for her. This, sadly, would inevitably lead to the undesired outcome manifesting. Had Paula chosen to have a positive mindset, things would undoubtedly have unfolded in her favor. Such is the power of our mindsets; they can either break us or build us up.

Differences Between a Growth and Fixed Mindset

The source of stagnation, discontent, pain, and living below your potential is having a fixed mindset. On the other hand, the source of growth, fulfillment, adventure, new experiences, and living up to your fullest potential is having a growth mindset. If such mindsets give us these contrasting realities, it's certainly worth learning how to discard a fixed mindset and adopt a growth mindset.

A growth mindset entails having the understanding and perception that skills, intelligence, new experiences, abilities, and talents can all be learned and improved through putting in the necessary effort. Conversely, having a fixed mindset entails believing that your intelligence, competence, abilities, and skills are innate and unchangeable.

For instance, someone who doesn't have a background in business management might avoid any opportunities to work in the entrepreneurship field because they believe that they will never excel in that field. Even though the rationale is understandable, the belief that one can never excel in business management before even trying is a counterproductive way of decoding reality.

Here are some key characteristics of someone with a growth mindset:

☞ Since they believe that their abilities can be developed, they are always open to learning and trying new things.

☞ She is very teachable and receptive to feedback.

☞ More open to taking risks.

☞ Procrastinate less and do things even when they don't feel ready for it.

☞ They are seldom content with doing things the same way; they are always looking for ways to improve.

☞ Tend to have more spontaneous, fun-filled, and adventurous lives filled with novelty.

☞ They are more likely to discover and unleash their fullest potential.

☞ Tend to have stronger relationships. They don't hold on to past hurts or grudges but rather focus on moving forward.

☞ They tend to survive high-pressure situations or environments because they believe that there is always a way around things.

☞ Tend to have healthy self-esteem, self-worth, and confidence.

Now, let's have a look at some key characteristics of a fixed mindset:

☞ Can often fall into cynical, hopeless, and negative ways of thinking.

☞ Hardly ever leave their comfort zone.

☞ I am apprehensive of feedback and often dismiss it. They can often ignore and mistrust others, which in turn causes a lot of interpersonal conflicts in their lives.

☞ Always afraid of anything outside of what they ordinarily do. Hardly try new things.

☞ Don't even try to reach out for new opportunities because they believe they can never be better than they currently are.

☞ They are not good listeners; they tend to be very attached to their perspective and set in their ways.

☞ Have trouble letting go of old hurts and believing that people can change?

☞ Can live a very boring lifestyle with the same routines even if they aren't serving them well.

☞ Hardly innovate new things. May settle for "what is" and never try to make performance improvements in anything.

☞ Hardly ever fulfill their esteem and self-actualization needs, such as pursuing their dreams, because they believe that they are doomed to fail even if they try.

☞ Can be very narrow-minded about themselves and others.

☞ May come across as very judgmental of people who aren't like them.

☞ Have the habit of constantly avoiding challenges.

☞ They often have a very loud negative self-talk voice that plants fear and hinders them from being positive.

☞ They are often their biggest bullies. They bully themselves into playing small and never allowing their true light to shine. They often discourage themselves through their counterproductive core beliefs and wrong assumptions.

☞ They struggle to achieve their goals more because they are not open to alternative, helpful ways to get things done successfully.

☞ They believe that their limitations and obstacles to success are permanent.

Benefits of a Growth Mindset

From the previous segment, it is clear that the longer one holds on to a fixed mindset, the more they will delay themselves from attracting abundance and unearthing their fullest potential.

☞ Since people with a growth mindset are always open to feedback, they tend to have greater competence and skills. They are always progressive, and this makes them relevant. In professional settings, it's difficult to replace or discard someone who is always growing and multi-talented.

☞ People with a growth mindset develop tenacity and grit. These qualities can only be there when you choose to see life differently. Just as the eagle has the tenacity to fly in the storm because it knows that the storm helps it to fly at the highest altitudes, similarly, you can also use your setbacks as a weapon to propel you forward.

☞ You will no longer be unsettled or emotionally dysregulated by change. Before embracing a growth mindset, change causes someone to feel anxious and petrified. All this can be a story of the past when you decide to accept that change is inevitable and can be used to your advantage.

☞ Being stuck with a fixed mindset can be utterly stressful. It's like living in a desert that used to have a little bit of precipitation until it started to dry out over time. You exhaust yourself and start being stressed about not having new things to put on the table. All this ends once you commit to being growth-oriented.

☞ You become free from the need to always chase after external validation. What matters to you is your daily progress rather than people's unhealthy expectations of you. A growth mindset allows you to break free from the need to always seek approval and ultimately silence your voice because you want to please others.

☞ Embracing a growth mindset will radically improve your relationships. People are always drawn to individuals who are great listeners. Things like hearing someone say, "I outgrew my relationship with them," become foreign to you. This is because you can never outgrow someone who is constantly improving themselves.

☞ Having a growth mindset improves your flexibility and adaptability in the face of situations that require you to act differently. This means that when obstacles and problems arise, you are likely to circumvent them wisely and rise above the storm.

☞ Staying in your comfort zone can be very depressing and emotionally distressing. When you embrace the growth mindset, you no longer have to deal with the issues of remaining stuck in your comfort zone.

☞ You can achieve your goals in any environment. A growth mindset allows you to meet your esteem and self-actualization needs. This makes you a happier and more content person.

☞ Adopting a growth mindset allows you to be a great team player because you respect other people's contributions and act on their feedback. This makes the team excel in its endeavors. There is no limit to the level of abundance one can attract when they have a growth mindset. You have more to give to others when you are always allowing your cup to be filled by keeping it open.

Even though the benefits of a growth mindset are very clear, without an understanding of how to apply it, one can remain stuck in their own fixed ways. To sort that out, here are some tips you can employ to make that transition to having an unwavering growth mindset.

☞ Make a list of everything you would love to try out, even the things that you are scared of. Start setting small, actionable goals for how you can begin to do those things step by step. If you need guidance on how to execute your wish list, ask the people who are good at it how they did it. Humility is one of the biggest assets someone with a fixed mindset can use to break free from their limited way of thinking. Don't be afraid to face your ignorance. Just accept what you don't know and reach out for help.

☞ Break free from your failure by learning to accept yourself. Most people with a fixed mindset are very self-critical. They usually accept themselves only when they think they are doing well. And when they aren't excelling, they may start to feel uncomfortable and ashamed of themselves. This causes them to only do things they are confident about and avoid what makes them uncomfortable. To break free from that, start loving and accepting yourself even during the times when you think you aren't doing so well. When you do that, others also begin to mirror that. They too start to accept you not only when you are the "perfect" person but also when you show your flaws and struggles. Thus, let yourself be unlimited, especially, when you are hitting rock bottom because of failure or taking new risks. Love yourself always.

☞ Change your perspective by always viewing challenges and limitations as opportunities for growth. In every seemingly dire situation, there is always good in it, but when you choose to focus on faults, that's all you will see.

☞ Have an accountability partner. People with a fixed mindset tend to rely heavily on their mindset. So break free from that pattern by allowing yourself to also value and trust other people's perspectives. An accountability partner can help you remember your worth, encourage you, and show you various ways to overcome any situation that you may not know how to deal with individually.

☞ Quit being hard on yourself and imposing unrealistic standards. Start celebrating your growth and every step of the journey instead of just postponing your happiness until the day you have achieved everything you want. Even if it's a small change you made one day, like waking up early when you know that you aren't a morning person. That's already a great growth step worth acknowledging and celebrating. Don't wait for you to do "everything right that day" before you can permit yourself to appreciate your growth.

☞ Always speak positively. Negative words come from a negative mindset. That sort of mindset is no longer your reality. Thus, each day you spend some time reinforcing positive thoughts and beliefs, be it through meditation or positive self-affirmations.

☞ Actively put yourself out there for new experiences. Be okay with having some form of discomfort for a while until you get accustomed to your new way of life. Become aware of the times when you resist change. Where you used to say no, consider saying yes this time and allowing yourself to tap into the unknown. The first few days are usually the hardest because your body will be trained to act in certain ways, even on autopilot. As you consistently do new things, you will also adjust, and it becomes less scary and much easier with time.

☞ Remember that problems and limitations are not meant to be perfect. Instead of rejecting opportunities because there is a problem, consider taking a different approach and asking others how you can fix that problem instead. When you maintain a seeking heart, answers eventually come to you. Thus, consider committing to no longer using excuses or problems as a scapegoat for your fear of trying new things.

☞ Reflect on the beliefs you have upheld about yourself up until now. Revise why those beliefs have controlled your life up until now. Recognize that you have the power to chart a new course today if you choose to. Uproot any negative core beliefs about your abilities. There are so many undiscovered versions of what you are capable of. Give yourself a chance to see the suppressed parts of who you are.

Understanding How Beliefs Impact You

Self-efficacy is a valuable attribute to cultivate when you want to unlock all of your potential. Just like self-belief, it is your deep-seated belief and confidence in your ability to successfully excel in achieving your goals or desired outcome. For instance, someone can have very high self-efficacy in their ability to attract their ideal romantic partner, excel in their exams, or land their dream career. However, it's also possible to have very low self-efficacy in some aspects of your life while having high self-efficacy in others. People with a fixed mindset tend to focus heavily on the areas they believe they are good at and then neglect areas they believe they will never be good at. This keeps them at the same level of success in their lives. It might work for a while, but as you grow older and meet more competent people, you can start to feel very insecure about yourself.

A perfect example of an animal that demonstrates a great level of self-efficacy is a lion. Lions believe that they can conquer any animal they are after. That is why they display the fearless attitude they have. If they didn't have such powerful self-efficacy, they would shrink in the face of other animals. That strong belief they have motivates them to chase after any prey that catches their eye. If that belief wasn't there, the lions would always play small and run away from their prey instead of seeing it as a potential tantalizing meal worth pursuing.

However, even though they have a fearless attitude when it comes to hunting, they still have low self-efficacy in other parts of their lives. For example, lions know very well that they aren't the best at navigating their way in big water bodies, which is why you seldom see them in the middle of rivers or oceans; you would typically always find them on land. But does that mean if lions didn't learn how to be champions in water bodies too, they wouldn't thrive there? Who knows? We can only know what their real limits are if they try.

Similarly, up until now, you may have had great self-efficacy in many areas of your life. But now it's time to break away from any limits and learn how to develop high self-efficacy in every aspect of your life. Believe that there is nothing impossible for you if only you try. To get there, we first need to have a clear understanding of where our belief systems lie. How do you perceive yourself, and what's your self-efficacy? You may use these questions to reflect on yourself and gain personal clarity about where you stand.

Self-Efficacy Strength Evaluation:

- ☞ Do you feel like your current job is the best job you can get this year? Is there any chance that if you search hard enough, you can land a better job?

- ☞ Do you quit and let go of your dreams when challenges storm in?

- ☞ Do you allow other people's opinions of you to determine how you perceive yourself?

- ☞ Are you composed and grounded when things don't go your way?

- ☞ Do you shrink under pressure or become like gold refined in a furnace?

- ☞ Do you focus on all the things you haven't achieved yet rather than what you already have?

- ☞ How confident are you about achieving your best goals?

- ☞ Do you believe that learning from others and putting in hard work can make you an even more capable person?

☞ Do you bounce back after being knocked down by life, or do you tend to stay down?

If your answers were yes or positive regarding most of these questions, then chances are that you have very healthy self-efficacy. However, if you were on the other end of the spectrum, chances are that you might be stuck with a fixed mindset. Thankfully, as you apply the strategies we spoke about, all that can now be in your past, and you can usher in a new era of the evolved version of yourself—someone with a strong and empowered sense of self-efficacy.

The best ways to deconstruct negative beliefs and foster new, healthier ones are to open yourself up to new experiences, use *social modeling* and *persuasion* to your advantage, and invest in *mastering emotional management.*

Opening yourself up to new experiences and allowing yourself to fail and learn as you go through the trial-and-error process allows you to hone your skills. As you repeatedly do the same things over time, your confidence and self-efficacy in those areas grow exponentially. This is why whenever anyone is learning how to drive, the best way is to let them learn how to drive even without prior experience. You just let them drive, even if they are terrified. Eventually, through practice, someone starts to believe that they can drive. That belief will be strong and grounded because it will be backed up by real-life, repeated experiences of driving successfully.

Have you ever had a friend who was barely good at something, but the moment they saw you doing it, they started believing that they too could do it? Their thinking would typically sound like this: *if so and so can do it, so can I.* They watch people rise and get better, and that too, can inspire them to get out of their shells. Similarly, ask yourself if it's fair to conclude that you specifically can't do something that many other people around you might already be doing. Next, challenge yourself and try it out too!

We all remember that one teacher in school who perhaps used to be very kind to us and say positive words of affirmation about our abilities. It is those people who alter our limited perspectives of ourselves and help us to believe in ourselves. Improve your self-efficacy by allowing your loved ones and people who know you very well to share with you the potential they see in you. Receiving words of encouragement is powerful and persuasive. Reading motivational and self-help books is all part of feeding yourself the edifying literature that breathes life into your spirit.

Have you ever noticed that emotions greatly influence the decisions we make and even how we feel about ourselves? If you feel terrible about yourself, being in that state for a prolonged period can start to influence you to believe that you can't rise above your current situation. Therefore, practice mindfulness and spend your time more in the present instead of the past or future. Worrying about the past and future can make it hard to be emotionally stable. Instead, you feel overwhelmed and end up believing that you can't control your current reality. As you train yourself to have less tolerance for negative emotions, you will build up your self-efficacy and strength.

Once your beliefs are corrected, and you make the decision to interpret life from a positive perspective, your beliefs stop hindering you from attracting the reality you want to see. You can also change your physiology and create a new set of positive beliefs. For instance, you can't believe that you are confident and expect others to take you seriously when you speak in a low voice, look down, and slouch. Your body language has to match what you believe about yourself. Even if you still don't feel like you believe in all the positive things you want to believe about yourself, what matters is taking action that matches the person you wish to become. Actions will reinforce the belief!

Interactive Exercise

To help you get started decluttering all your negative beliefs, you can take some time to write down everything beautiful and empowering you would love to represent you.

Next, brainstorm about all the practical things you can start doing to match those new beliefs. Thereafter, start acting according to that blueprint. As you stay in character for a long time, that new version of yourself eventually becomes the real you.

Consider taking some time each day to meditate and have a clear vision of who you want to be. Imagine how you will take the steps necessary to get there. Also, create space in your mind to critique any negative thoughts instead of just impulsively believing them. The more distance you create between your negative thoughts and the self-aware new you, the less powerful those thoughts will be.

Take time to forgive yourself during your meditation sessions. Forgive yourself for every missed opportunity when you used to have a fixed mindset. Let go of the past. Thereafter, focus on cultivating gratitude for your awakening now and all the limitless opportunities waiting for you as you fully embrace the growth mindset. Ready to start living life to the fullest? I earnestly believe you are.

Now that we have explored the various aspects of having a growth or fixed mindset, I'm sure you are excited to implement the necessary changes in your life. However, what you will notice is that one of the most difficult things to do is to become fully self-aware. It's easy to know others very well, but often, people are very oblivious about themselves. This makes the prospect of effective change difficult to instill. Thankfully, the next chapter will help you thoroughly prepare for those obstacles and overcome them. You will learn how to be self-aware, and this will protect you from standing in the way of your happiness any longer.

Chapter 2

Becoming Self-Aware

It took me decades to finally come to terms with the fact that the happiness we might have spent years chasing after was probably closer to us than we thought. If you've ever watched an animated movie called "Soul," you would understand an important lesson about happiness. In that movie, the main character was a jazz middle school teacher. He lived most of his life believing that his "spark" and what would make him truly happy was landing a career in the music field as a jazz pianist.

He lived most of his life feeling like things went wrong and regretting the life he had created for himself. He just wanted to make things right. One day, he found himself in the afterlife, where he had to help a colleague he met there find his spark. He was devastated to see that he had "died" and wanted to go back to earth to fulfill his dream of being a jazz musician. He had an opportunity to audition for the role of a jazz pianist just before he was taken to the other realm. Fast forward: He managed to finally attend the audition, and after landing his dream job that he thought would make him happy and complete, he was puzzled by something. He thought that finally getting this one thing he believed would make him happy would radically change his life and give him the happy ending he believed in. However, the reality was far from that. He didn't get the sense of fulfillment or happiness he thought he would. This left him devastated. This was a man who was often distraught and hardly present for other things. All he cared about all his life was jazz. Then, when he got the chance to make his dream come true, he realized that even that didn't give him the fulfillment he believed he would get.

When he shared his feelings with the lady who hired him, she understood where he was coming from. She told him about the story of a fish that lived most of its life, asking to see or have the ocean. That fish believed that the best thing that could happen to it was being in an ocean. That's when the fish was told that it was already in the ocean. Then the fish insisted that no, it wasn't the ocean; it was just the water it was in.

Even though the fish was indeed in the ocean all along, its perception of reality hindered it from realizing that it already had everything it was looking for. It just had to change its outlook and learn to recognize, accept, and appreciate what it already had. It's by embracing that truth that happiness will be attained. However, for as long as the fish kept believing that it didn't have what it needed to be happy and fulfilled, then it would just live most of its life searching for the ocean and unable to enjoy its present life. Similarly, this too, is the lesson the middle school teacher learned: That happiness is not just found in the one thing we believe will make us happy. It's already all around you. You will find it when you learn to appreciate life and make the most of every step of your journey. It's found in being grateful for everything you already have and not taking for granted how other people contribute their light and love to you already.

When I watched this movie, I didn't expect myself to shed a tear. However, the story was so powerful because this is exactly how most people live their lives. They postpone their happiness and choose to believe that happiness will only come if they attend a certain school, get a certain qualification or degree, land a particular job, or have a relationship, amongst many other assumptions. As a result, many people live most of their lives devoid of happiness. They take for granted what they already have and waste years of their lives stuck in misery and wishful thinking. They become unaware of how they can make the most of their strengths today and overcome their weaknesses. They downplay themselves and live lives that hardly reflect their true potential for success.

Perhaps when you were in elementary school, you spent most of your days wishing to be a teenager because you thought that stage was more fun. Then, when you became a teenager and saw all the challenges of adolescence, you started wishing to be an adult and shut yourself off from leveraging the growth opportunities that you had at that stage. Once you became an adult, you may have felt like what would make you happy was being married and having babies. Once you had the family, perhaps you were shocked to realize that the problems didn't stop; in fact, maybe you had more issues than ever before. The cycle keeps going on and on until you decide to change your mindset and reframe your reality.

When we are aware of how we think, it helps us to discard thought patterns and behaviors that no longer serve us. However, people who are oblivious to what causes them to suffer continue to do things that add pain to their lives instead of eliminating it. Therefore, this chapter will help you to have some time and guidance in deeply reflecting on who you have been up until now. Once you are mindful of your patterns and what you can do to take charge of your happiness instead of waiting for it to be handed to you, you set yourself free. By doing so, you will be able to start living a full life with meaning and purpose. Developing a successful mindset takes work, but the reward is having infinite wealth and happiness every day, not just someday in the future.

Do You Have a Fixed or Growth Mindset?

In this section, I would like you to take some time to identify if you have a fixed or growth mindset. What would you say is your primary mindset? Maybe some days and in some situations, you display a growth mindset. But perhaps for the most part, you usually have a fixed mindset as your default setting. If you already have primarily a growth mindset, try to identify areas in your life where you may need to apply that growth mindset where you didn't before. There is always room for improvement, so no matter how strong your mindset might be, allow yourself to keep progressing and charting new courses you may not have discovered before.

What often brings us the most suffering in our lives is when we feel like we aren't growing. Perhaps your grades at school or college are always in the same range, or at work, you always have that average position; or in your relationships, you often have a repetition of the same frustrating relationship dynamics, or in your life, you follow the same old routine that doesn't inspire and excite you anymore. What are the areas where you feel like you are not growing?

The main reason why you might be experiencing stagnation in those areas is because the fixed mindset has been taking the reigns over you. Or perhaps you do have a growth mindset but have just fallen into a pattern of complacency and slothfulness.

Now, let's review some of the main elements of how someone with a growth mindset functions and views situations. People with a growth mindset tend to

☞ believe that there is so much they can do. Their gifts and talents are not limited to what they know. They believe that with effort and time, their talents can grow, and they can learn new skills.

☞ be very optimistic. They have a positive attitude when approaching different situations. They are likely to succeed more because of their positive attitude.

☞ always seek opportunities for growth and self-improvement. They are open to learning and reinventing themselves to be better people.

☞ see mistakes and defeats as valuable life lessons to help them improve. They don't use mistakes as a weapon to talk themselves down. Hence, mistakes hardly make them feel insecure or afraid to keep trying.

☞ not hide from challenges. They don't call it quits when life gets hard. Instead, they believe that there is always a way to overcome. Thus, they are more likely to ask for help or remain tenuous in the face of adversity. They often derive the courage to fight harder from the setbacks they face.

☞ not settle for average. They keep honing their skills until they achieve mastery.

☞ not compare themselves to others in unhealthy ways. They don't feel threatened by other people's success; instead, it inspires them to do better.

☞ be receptive to feedback. Be it good or bad, they find a way to use all the information they receive to better themselves.

☞ have more exciting lives full of new experiences and unlimited growth.

From the above characteristics of someone with a fixed mindset, which points did you identify with? What do you think your life would be like if you didn't think that way? What do you think you could have achieved by now? Why do you think this is the reason for your mindset being this way? Write down your answers as you reflect on all these questions. What matters is being honest with yourself and having clarity about how you show up in this world.

Now, let's review some of the main elements of how someone with a growth mindset functions and views situations. People with a growth mindset tend to:

- ☞ believe that there is so much they can do. Their gifts and talents are not just limited to what they know. They believe that with effort and time, their talents can grow, and they can learn new skills.

- ☞ be very optimistic. They have a positive attitude when approaching different situations. They are likely to succeed more because of their positive attitude.

- ☞ always seek opportunities for growth and self-improvement. They are open to learning and reinventing themselves to be better people.

- ☞ see mistakes and defeat as valuable life lessons to help them improve. They don't use mistakes as a weapon to talk themselves down. Hence, mistakes hardly make them feel insecure or afraid to keep trying.

- ☞ not hide from challenges. They don't call it quits when life gets hard. Instead, they believe that there is always a way to overcome. Thus, they are more likely to ask for help or remain tenuous in the face of adversity. They often derive the courage to fight harder from the setbacks they face.

☞ not settle for average. They keep honing their skills until they achieve mastery.

☞ not compare themselves to others in unhealthy ways. They don't feel threatened by other people's success; instead, it inspires them to do better.

☞ be receptive to feedback. Be it good or bad, they find a way to use all the information they receive to better themselves.

☞ have more exciting lives full of new experiences and unlimited growth.

How to Shift From a Fixed Mindset to a Growth Mindset

The first step towards shifting from having a fixed mindset to embracing a growth mindset is to be fully aware of yourself. Reflecting on the patterns you see in your life—how you think, talk, and act—can help you have a clear understanding of where you are so that you can discard the habits that keep you stuck in the fixed mindset zone.

Once you have written down all the things you perceive about your current behavioral patterns, you will be ready to recreate your life.

The following steps can guide you on ways you can let go of the old you and embrace the growth-oriented, upgraded version of yourself. Let's now have a look at those action steps:

☞ Write a blueprint of all the things you would like to achieve and become. Use your unrestrained imagination.

☞ Commit to stop thinking about what others think of you or seeking their validation. Instead, focus more on seeking approval and respect from yourself. You can only get that when you stop sabotaging yourself and begin to go after what you want. Waiting for others to approve of you prevents you from embracing the growth mindset. You avoid doing things because of the fear that people will mock or laugh at you if you fail.

☞ Commit to start showing up as your true self. Embracing authenticity and accepting all of who you are frees you to be yourself. Don't just accept the ideal version of yourself you are working towards. Start accepting who you are now and let your love for that person motivate you to be your best self.

☞ Stop listening to negative thoughts. Often, what keeps people stuck in a fixed mindset is being too attached to negative thoughts. Dare to challenge every "I can't" you have and replace it with "Of course I can."

☞ Use criticism as a tool to build yourself up. When we see criticism as an attack, we always avoid it by all means possible. Unfortunately, this can make you ignorant about important things that can help you grow. Therefore, start being open to any form of criticism, see if there is any truth in it, and humbly accept it. This does not mean that you should condone disrespectful behavior. You still have been teaching people to communicate with you respectfully. However, think carefully about what people say and use their relevant insights to build yourself up.

☞ Appreciate and enjoy the journey of evolving into your best self. When someone has a fixed mindset, they are usually set on only being happy after they achieve their goal. Reverse that way of thinking and now begin to appreciate every step of your growth process. Laugh at your mistakes, find humor in the silly things you do, and just accept yourself. Don't be afraid to take risks in front of others; this will help you earn people's respect as they observe your courage. By valuing the process of your development, you allow others to also appreciate and celebrate you at every stage of your growth journey.

☞ Believe that you can be good at anything as long as you put your mind to it. Instead of ruling yourself out as being bad at doing something, start changing your language and saying, "I'm not yet good at that." This keeps the possibility of you learning and mastering anything you set your mind to open.

☞ Ask for help. Relying on your intelligence alone will not help you grow your skills. Start to reach out for help. This is a realistic way to learn many new things.

☞ Maintain a positive attitude. Start being mindful of your language and attitude. Where you used to be negative and cynical, start practicing optimism. When opportunities knock, be the first to say "yes" to them.

☞ Be disciplined. It's so easy to be negative and avoid growing. The comfort zone is what it is... comfortable. So, start escaping your comfort zone by practicing discipline and being consistent in showing up for yourself. Train your body and mind to follow your goals and not be held back by temporary feelings of discouragement. You can do this by using positive affirmations every day.

☞ Challenge yourself to do at least two new things each day. One for yourself and the other for others. This keeps you growing in your relationships with yourself and others.

☞ Continue to expose yourself to content or any opportunities that help you disengage from your old pattern. Most negative ways of thinking are rooted in adverse childhood experiences. To foster sustainable transformation, consider investing in healing from old wounds and reframing your beliefs. This ensures that the impact of any unfavorable past experiences you had won't keep holding you back.

Assess and Be Mindful of All Your Strengths and Weaknesses

Someone who doesn't know how powerful they are can be a victim of almost anything. It would be rare to see a lion running away from a hyena or giraffe because it is fully aware of its capacity to fight those animals if there is ever a need to. Likewise, when we don't know how powerful we are, we can continue to run away from challenges that we have the fortitude to overcome.

Have you ever felt like you keep running away from problems that, by now, you should have at least mastered how to overcome easily? Growing older won't guarantee that what you used to struggle with will suddenly go away. Many people are often surprised by this as they get older. Nothing changes unless you change your approach to life.

To help you exercise bravery and no longer be inflicted sorrowfully with the same old issues, begin to have a full assessment of all your strengths and weaknesses. This enables you to exercise your power instead of hiding it when life calls for you to do so. It also allows you to invest your time in working on your weaknesses so that they don't remain your weaknesses for years.

People are gifted with all kinds of strengths. Let's explore the examples of strengths you might have in your life:

Social life (interpersonal skills)

- ☞ Being a great listener

- ☞ Being empathic and sensitive to others

- ☞ Being compassionate

- ☞ Being Kindness

- ☞ Being a great networker

- ☞ Being a great storyteller

- ☞ Being fun or easy-going

- ☞ Being a good communicator

Intellectual Skills

- ☞ Being a fast learner

- ☞ Being a creative person

- ☞ Being an articulate and eloquent communicator

- ☞ Being good at researching

- ☞ Being a great innovator

- ☞ Being good with numbers or words

Emotional Intelligence

- ☞ Being able to understand other people's feelings

- ☞ Being able to decode and regulate your own emotions

- ☞ Being able to effectively communicate your feelings and needs

- ☞ Being able to be present for others or ask others to be present for you

- ☞ Being warm and loving

Restraint

- ☞ Being able to refrain from gossip even when tempted to engage

- ☞ Being able to discern what's good from bad and choosing the right path

- ☞ Being able to avoid substances and bad diets

- ☞ Being able to push yourself to exercise and take care of your body even when you don't feel like it

- ☞ Being patient with others

- ☞ Being loyal even in the face of tempting prospects

- ☞ Being able to avoid procrastination and distractions

Spiritual Virtues (Theological)

☞ Being a faithful person

☞ Being self-controlled

☞ Being good-hearted

☞ Being considerate of others

☞ Being passionate

☞ Being morally upright

☞ Being strong-willed

☞ Being wise and prudent

☞ Being a forgiving person who encourages unity and not division among people

Common weaknesses that people often struggle with are:

☞ Being too outspoken and inconsiderate of others' feelings

☞ Lacking empathy and sympathy for others

☞ Laziness and lack of discipline

☞ Fear of social engagements and making new friends

☞ Being self-absorbed

☞ Worrying too much

☞ Being constantly pessimistic

☞ Communicating rudely with others

☞ Procrastinating or avoiding responsibility

☞ Failing to assertively communicate your needs and resorting to aggression instead

☞ Being too judgmental and critical of others while turning a blind eye to your faults

☞ Being unreliable and tardy

Using the above examples, write down everything you can relate to and also add other strengths and weaknesses you have not included.

Knowing your strengths helps you to appreciate and love yourself more. It allows you to also fulfill your purpose and serve others better. By taking your strengths and not downplaying them, you will be able to finally embrace the growth mindset.

It's hard to understand why people react the way they do to you when you aren't aware of your weaknesses. When they show you how your behavior is affecting them, you are likely to be defensive instead of grateful for learning about what's wrong and changing it. Therefore, being self-aware undoubtedly helps you to understand others and build meaningful, lasting relationships with them.

Interactive Exercise

Take time to also identify the opportunities you have for growing and becoming a better person. List those opportunities and start making goals about how you can leverage them. Your goals have to be measurable, specific, and realistic. Break them down into short-, medium-, and long-term goals for what you want to achieve. This will help you to make actionable plans that you can review each day.

Never forget that your mindset can change. Just as muscles grow bigger by consistently exercising, so will your growth mindset also develop when you continue to challenge yourself. Just imagine how thrilling your life will start to become as you allow your wings to spread and fly to places you have always been scared of going. Now is the time; don't clip your wings any longer.

As you prepare for your famous flight and soar with a growth mindset, there are many challenges you are bound to face. This next chapter will teach you how to prepare and handle them with resilience and unwavering determination.

Chapter 3

Embracing Challenges With Persistence and Resilience

Stories have a wonderful and inspiring way of uplifting our spirits and motivating us to make the right choices in life. Have you ever heard of the "Potato, Egg, and Coffee Beans" story?

This is how the story goes: A young lady felt despondent in life. She was utterly fed up with the day-to-day struggle of being a human being. All the cares and worries of life felt exhausting to her. She decided to confide in her mother and ask for help. She unburdened her heart and shared how tired and burned out she was from constantly fighting and struggling through life. She was honest about her lack of motivation to keep going.

Her wise mother decided to practically illustrate to her an important lesson to help her reframe her mindset and stir up tenacity in her child's spirit. She took three pots and filled them with the same amount of water. Thereafter, she put the potatoes, egg, and coffee beans in the three pots separately.

She brought all her ingredients to a boil, and after a few minutes, she took the pots off the stove to cool down. Upon observing the changes that had transpired for each ingredient, they all had different reactions to the same conditions. Before the potato was put to a boil, it was firm and sturdy. But after being boiled for a while, it became soft and very weak. It could break easily.

Before the egg was put to a boil, it was fragile. But after being boiled for a while, it becomes hardened and firm.

Prior to adding the coffee beans to the water and boiling them, they were as usual and intact. After boiling them, they didn't necessarily lose their value but rather transformed into something better. They managed to change the water into a robust, aromatic, and tasty coffee.

Thereafter, the young lady's mother explains to her troubled daughter the main lesson behind what just happened. She showed her how, despite facing the same adversity as boiling water, each of the three objects had different reactions.

The potato was initially strong, but adversity turned it into a weak and soft food item. The egg was initially fragile, but once it faced adversity, it became hard and firm. The coffee beans had an incredible reaction to adversity. They used their challenge to create something different and even more desirable.

It was clear to the young lady that it's not our struggles that are the main problem. Instead, what holds us back and brings us so much misery is our perspective and how we choose to react to situations. She too, had the choice to either react like the potatoes, eggs, or coffee beans.

Up until now, what sort of object from the aforementioned three resembles you the most? Are you someone who shrinks back and becomes weak when adversity strikes? Perhaps you are like the egg that becomes hardened after going through difficulties. Or maybe you now want to be like the coffee beans, who were able to graciously adapt to their situation and use it to their advantage to create something more valuable...

What's important to note is that adversity is inevitable. We all have times when life will most certainly throw us challenges that may make us lose faith in ourselves. If that has been you all along, now you have a chance to reframe your mindset and develop an empowered way of dealing with hardships. Did you know that wind can make some trees break while others become stronger because of the effect of the wind?

In this chapter, we will explore how you can become resilient in any hard situation in life. Waiting for everything to be "perfect" before you choose to be happy is merely a false dream to sell yourself. The true winners in life are people who learn to use the storms in their lives to soar even higher than before. People see problems as opportunities for success instead of threats. Thus, they embrace struggles with a positive frame of mind, and that allows them to keep winning no matter what befalls them.

If you are tired of having intermittent and sporadic success and now want to consistently do great, you're at the right place. Today, you will understand the art of being a champion amid the cold seasons of your life. When you learn how to shine your light, especially during unexpectedly difficult times, you begin to take charge of your life. No longer will you remain a victim of difficult situations. Instead, just as gold becomes refined through being put in a furnace, you too will unleash the best versions of yourself during times of hardship and struggle.

Delineating the Importance of Challenges

Benefits of challenges:

☞ **Help you to build relationships**: When adversity strikes, relying on yourself alone can make things worse. Hence, challenges put you in a position where you learn to accept other people's significance and contribution to your life. They allow us to learn how to connect and socially engage with others. This in turn, has many more benefits, such as no longer lacking company, having people who care about you to confide in, and learning how to maintain healthy dependence.

☞ **They push you to unleash your potential**: When you have no reason to leave your comfort zone, you remain the same person and get comfortable with the same achievements. However, once adversity hits you, it can push you to unleash and discover your hidden strengths. You get to see things you are capable of that you possibly never thought you would be able to do. Thus, the more you overcome your setbacks, the more fulfilled and accomplished you become.

☞ **Challenges grow your self-efficacy**: Have you ever thought you couldn't do something, then one day you are pushed to do that thing you always feared? Once you successfully do it, the fear you used to have suddenly disappears. You start being more confident about your ability to get things done and overcome similar challenges. This is what self-efficacy is. Your belief and confidence in your ability to crush any goals and face your fears. This is why, when people are afraid of something, it's always best to expose them to that thing until they develop confidence in their ability to navigate through things successfully. For example, if someone is hydrophobic and doesn't want to swim, the only way that fear will disappear is if they keep trying to swim. Once they master how to swim, their efficacy will have grown with regard to their ability to swim.

☞ **They can compel you to accept post-traumatic growth**: If you are someone with a dark past and have gone through so much hurt, it can be hard to maintain positivity. Sometimes, what happens to you may trigger and put more salt on your old wounds. Other times, you may notice that your challenge is that you keep attracting the same painful experiences. Eventually, you would have to face your past and invest in growing yourself so that you don't keep repeating patterns that don't serve you. Thus, the more you face the same issues, the more likely you are to start accepting that something is wrong. Once the problem is acknowledged, you will be able to foster growth to prevent yourself from keeping on reliving your past.

☞ **Challenges prevent idleness and complacency**: When you are faced with a situation that demands you rise to the occasion, you are likely to think more on your feet. Challenges are known to keep people's minds sharp. They push you to use your skills and ideas to solve problems. This is good as it allows you to continue growing and learning new things.

☞ **Helps with developing empathy**: If you haven't faced what it's like to be critically ill, you may struggle to show practical sympathy and empathy to someone ill. If you were once poor and now you are rich, you are likely to have empathy for people who are still battling with poverty because you would know what it's like to be in that position. Thus, challenges help us to be empathetic and deeply connect with others. They provide us with the wisdom we need to physically and emotionally support people who need us.

☞ **They build resilience and grit**: Just like the egg that hardens when boiled, you too, can develop mental toughness when put in difficult situations.

Your environment can help you have skills that you would never be able to have by merely theoretically trying to understand how to have them. This mental toughness and grit can help you for the rest of your life. Where people easily give up, you remain standing. You become resilient and can successfully adapt to dire circumstances without faltering.

☞ **You get to enjoy the rewards of winning**: Without overcoming some sort of challenge, it's impossible to be a champion in life. Athletes train so hard to win the world championship post. It can be strenuously challenging to endure all that they have to go through before that. However, those challenges can never stop them from enjoying the rewards of their hard work once the time comes. Thus, you too will get a chance to enjoy the rewards of your hard work and sweat if you dare not give up. Challenges also help you learn how to regulate your emotions and be disciplined. This, in turn, benefits every other aspect of your life.

From reviewing the lives of most people we see overcoming challenges, it is evident that without them, they would have never given birth to the better versions of themselves.

Being a CEO, leader, doctor, or any profession requires mental fortitude. The more you don't run away from facing challenges in your area of responsibility, the more you invite more abundance into your life. During hardships, our eyes are open to the things we used to take for granted, and this cultivates gratitude. What time in your life do you feel that you faced one of your most difficult challenges, but it helped you become a better person? Let the memory of that story inspire you to keep embracing challenges with a positive and open mind.

Research determines that embracing the struggle and developing a growth mindset is what society needs (Spector, 2019). Professor Jo Boaler shared some insights about the importance of being receptive to learning. In her commentaries, she mentioned that believing that you can't hone a certain skill undermines your ability to learn. Many people claim that they are only good at certain things like "math" or "literacy," and those labels alone make it hard for them to be progressive learners. Instead of embracing the struggle of learning something new until they master it, they would rather just stick to the few things they think they are good at.

She also added that sometimes parents and teachers tend to label children as "smart," and that can be detrimental. The reason behind her rationale was that when someone thinks they are smart, it can get in the way of their being open to learning new things. When they fail, the message they can instill in themselves may be that "I'm not smart after all." As a result, this can fracture someone's self-esteem and self-efficacy. What is suggested as a better way to maintain an openness to learning is complimenting students by saying things like, "I loved the creative solution you used to that problem," or "You solved that problem very well." Such language allows people to believe that there are infinite possibilities for how they can improve their intelligence. However, if you tell someone that they are smart, it can make the person stuck in a fixed mindset and not grow beyond the label you gave them. As a result, that fixed way of thinking will make it hard for them to adapt to situations that they deem to not be in their area of expertise.

Another point she made was the importance of allowing people to embrace the struggle when they can't figure things out. So when someone says something like, "I'm finding this hard," it's advised to acknowledge that reality and let them know that it's fantastic that they are facing challenges. If challenges are demonized and perceived as "bad things" all the time, it makes it hard for people to derive the good from those challenges. It makes it hard for them to be open to the growth that's waiting for them if they embrace the struggle. Hence, start celebrating people even before they triumph. Appreciate people for sticking through their challenges and show them that by choosing to face their battles, they have already started to win and will never be the same.

In psychology, mental toughness is known to be achieved when you can maintain your flow state for prolonged periods. "Flow state" is that zone you are in when you can get things done, and you are fully engaged in what needs to be done. That flow state usually becomes hard to get into when adversity strikes due to emotions and difficult feelings. This is why working on being a disciplined person can help you achieve mental toughness. You know that you have mental toughness when these attributes become the prevailing personality traits you have: self-control, confidence, commitment, and embracing challenges (Horikoshi, 2022).

Building Unwavering Resilience to Overcome Challenges

Having stamina and resilience go hand in hand. For example, when athletes can maintain the same amount of effort for a specific time during their races, that's stamina. On the other hand, resilience is when you can push forward and allow adversity to swallow you up into failure mode. Adversity might strike at any time and can go on for an indefinite period. It is being able to keep moving forward despite having all sorts of reasons why you could have given up. It's inevitable to face interruptions in your lane. It's possible to have unforeseen challenges emerge from nowhere. Therefore, resilience is what is needed to keep your eyes on what matters and not let go of your goals because of hardship.

Let's now unpack the various ways you can build your resilience muscles:

☞ **Break up your responsibility into small, manageable tasks**: Your mind and body need time to get momentum and into the flow of getting things done. This is why pacing yourself by setting small goals before tackling the bigger ones is extremely important. Whenever you complete your small task, it will increase your confidence and inspire you to do even more. This is how you can create mental fortitude to handle bigger goals.

Always remember to use a checklist and start the day with smaller tasks until you have the strength to face the bigger responsibilities.

☞ **Build and maintain a caring, supportive structure**: It's one thing to have people in your life and another to have reliable relationships. When adversity strikes, that's when you need the support of other people too. It's important to invest in nurturing worthwhile relationships with people who won't flake in your time of need. This can be done by also extending your help to others when they need you. That way, it becomes more probable that they are likely to also extend their hand to you when challenges strike. Just knowing that you're not alone amid the challenges you are facing will help you to have resilience and persevere.

☞ **Always be mindful of things to be grateful about**: There is always something good about seemingly difficult situations. What can help you have resilience and not give in to the pressure of giving up is always having a grateful heart. When you look for faults and things to complain about, that's all you will find. However, when you focus on finding the good in every situation, you become aware of the vast things you can be grateful for. It's when the mind is constantly negative that moving forward starts to feel pointless.

☞ **Celebrate and take credit for what you have already achieved**: Remembering how far you have come can help you resurrect your self-trust and self-belief. Keep a success journal where you can record all your accomplishments. During the times when you are battling to believe in yourself, take some time to review all the battles you have already won. This will help you remember how powerful you are, and as a result, resilience will be strengthened.

☞ **Embrace change**: What's predictable feels safe and comfortable to us as human beings. However, life is all about changes, and time never stops ticking. Just as we have to adjust to changing seasons and dress accordingly, so do you. You also have to adjust your mind to the changes happening in your life. Accepting that change is part of life and that there is always a way to show up wisely in different situations will help you foster resilience. Accepting change helps you escape the victim mentality, and you will be able to live from a place of optimism and gratitude.

Making Amends With the Past, Embracing, and Learning From Failure

When we fail to meet our expectations, feelings of worthlessness and defeat can almost suffocate us. However, once you choose to look at failure differently, you will never continue to let it hinder you from trying new things.

Many people fail to achieve their goals and reach places they wish to because of the fear of failure. What exactly is failure, though? What about it makes it seem so difficult to bear that sometimes we are willing to sabotage ourselves and say goodbye to our dreams?

Failure is when you perceive that what you did didn't match your expected favorable outcome. What often makes failure sting so badly is the interpretation we give it. If you perceive failure as an opportunity for progression, learning, and maturity, it becomes a positive thing. However, if your understanding of failure is that it is a shameful thing that ought to be avoided by all means possible, chances are that you would live most of your life walking on eggshells to avoid making any mistakes. This can be an exhausting way to navigate through life.

When you fail, how do you often interpret that failure? Do you believe that your failures define you? Do you think they make your worth and significance as a human any less?

For many people who fear failure, life is often a repetition of the same old things that are familiar and safe. The comfort zone is primarily the place where people who fear failure live in. In that zone, nothing new grows, and this can lead to feelings of being stuck or stagnant in life.

Perhaps up until now, you allowed failure to be your enemy instead of an ally. You can shift your paradigm and redefine failure so that you can embrace it as part of your process of evolving into the best version of yourself you are meant to be.

Therefore, here are some keyways you can change your narrative about failure:

- ☞ Failure is necessary for me to grow and reach my fullest potential.

- ☞ If I am not failing many times each day, it probably means that I am not trying any new things and testing my limits.

- ☞ Failure is not a bad thing; it is part of what allows us to discover more intelligent ways of doing things.

- ☞ Failure does not define who I am; it merely shows me how much I am willing to try and allows me to improve my resilience.

- ☞ What people think of me is not my problem or business; it is what l think of myself that matters the most. And I think I am very brave to have tried so many things in my life, even though some experiences didn't turn out the way l would have wanted them to. What counts is that I learned something.

Interactive Exercise

1. Name five things you always avoided doing but deep down your heart knew that you were supposed to.

2. Create an activity plan with a daily to-do list of all the new things you would like to do to start facing your fears.

3. Is there anyone good at a specific skill you have always wanted to master? Schedule a meeting with that person the following week and share with them your interest in growing and learning from them.

4. What are your main strengths, and how have you developed them?

5. What have you always wanted to be? Write down your ideal, best version of yourself and start getting into character from today! The more you practice being the new you, the faster that becomes your new identity and in no time!

This chapter has shown you that going forward, there is no reason why you should ever be afraid of failing or see your past failures as something to be ashamed of. Start owning your mistakes and confidently carrying yourself even in times when things don't go as expected. This is the true essence of being "alive," refusing to merely exist!

Chapter 4

Cultivate a Love for Learning

Lifelong learning entails the self-initiated acquisition of knowledge and understanding about anything of interest to you. The main goal behind it is to actively invest in your personal development and education. It can take place formally or informally. We live in a day and age where the world we are in is constantly changing at the speed of lightning. The digital technology revolution is impacting our way of life at an alarming pace than ever before. Just a few years ago, people hardly knew anything about AI technology. But now it's the talk of the day and those who turn a blind eye to it risk falling far behind in competence. Who would have ever thought that someone could think of making a car that drives itself? But today, the Tesla car was invented, and it's now a normal thing. Many countries already have cabs that drive themselves and operate transportation services. First, we used to use candles and lamps. Then people moved to use solar power, then people discovered the magic of electricity, and the inventions never ceased. Why is our society constantly changing? It's because people's knowledge is becoming extensive with time, and this enables them to create and invent all sorts of better things to use for our daily needs.

The time of assuming that learning was just for a season is now over. Even after getting your degree, it doesn't have to stop. Those who stop learning just because they have attained their tertiary education qualification are more likely to fall drastically behind in their skill level.

We are living in a very exciting time where information is no longer as scarce as it used to be. Internet access has become a lot easier for many people, allowing them to have the opportunity to enhance their education.

When someone has a fixed mindset, they stick to the belief that they are only what they already know. However, people with a growth mindset acknowledge that there is so much more they are yet to discover about themselves and be good at. Just that open-minded way of thinking promotes lifelong learning.

Our potential as a human being is not finite. We have limitless potential to achieve unthinkable heights. Hence, the idea of settling for mediocrity and being close-minded about learning is a huge disservice to oneself and those you could have helped.

Can you think of a story or example of someone in your life that you would consider a lifelong learner? How did that person's life turn out? It's most likely that their mindset helped them achieve a dazzling degree of unending success.

When children are raised to believe that they can learn and master any skill, it makes them not be afraid of failure or see it as a final destination. Their curiosity is encouraged, and they end up growing up into well-rounded adults. Children are very curious by nature. As they are growing, everything around them is new and fascinating. They hardly hold their mistakes against themselves as they explore the world. This open mind allows them to learn very fast, even way faster than adults at the time. Just think about how a child grows to master a language. All they do is keep an open mind, observe people around them, and mimic what they see and hear. In no time, they become good at replicating what they observe because they never stop learning.

Somewhere down the line of growing up, this learning and fast-paced development starts to slow down. When people adopt fixed beliefs and thoughts, it hinders them from nurturing that explorative mind. As a result, you start seeing people battle with limiting beliefs and then fail to see the myriad opportunities for growth and development that they used to see when they were younger.

Thankfully, by choosing to be a lifelong learner, you can reverse that and resurrect the curious and explorative part of yourself. True fulfillment in life comes when we allow ourselves to always grow. Stagnation gets boring. True adventure is only found when one is experiencing progress in one's life.

Lifelong learning can take place anywhere. It's never limited to classroom education. Think about the time you first learned how to make eggs from watching your mom cook... or perhaps the day you learned how to ride a bike. Think about when someone discovered a serene town library and went there to get a romance novel that shaped the romantic notions they started to have about life. And how about when people learn how to use chopsticks for the first time or speak a different language during their visits to other countries? With YouTube now being one of the most educational platforms for many life lessons, there is no end to what people can learn. Maybe you know someone who managed to get their dream body shape by following the homework videos posted there. Perhaps no one ever taught you how to cook, and you suddenly realized how essential that skill was when you were starting your family. Watching the cooking videos online or grabbing some cooking books must have saved the day. The point is that there are endless opportunities for lifelong learning. All that's needed is for someone to be mindful of them and intentional about making the most of every chance they get to grow their skills.

Things to remember about lifelong learning are that it is often self-initiated and doesn't always have to happen only when you have funds. You can do it free of charge, depending on what you are pursuing. What keeps you motivated to continue learning is your passion for self-development and seeing greater versions of yourself. You already have the natural drive to grow and improve the quality of your life. Tap into that desire and harness it to create the life of your dreams by embracing lifelong learning.

The Importance of Lifelong Learning

The benefits of lifelong learning are endless. Let's review some of them:

☞ **It improves your self-confidence and self-efficacy**: Do you remember how you used to feel whenever you knew that you'd successfully done something before and were asked to do it again? You would probably feel very confident about yourself and trust in your ability to complete the task at hand. This shows the significance of learning to help us build our self-efficacy and self-confidence. Would you want to apply for a job you know nothing about? Or offer to go surfing when you are clueless about good swimming techniques? Not. Learning helps you face your fears and limitations, overcome them, and then do what you love. It helps you build self-trust. The more you learn, the more your confidence becomes rock-solid.

☞ **It enhances your professional and personal skills**: Learning helps you to be a well-rounded person professionally and personally. School may provide you with textbook knowledge of certain subjects, but life requires you to know more than what schools provide. For example, learning how to be a good parent, how to build healthy relationships, or how to heal from your childhood trauma and wounds. All that knowledge is usually acquired through other forms of educational sources as you grow older. The more you research those topics and continue to grow your understanding, the better you become as a person. You can overcome your flaws and build helpful interpersonal skills that will improve your relationships both at home and at work.

☞ **It renews your passion for life**: Our lives can feel rather tiresome and draining when we are stuck in the same reality. This way of living can be exhausting and make you cynical about things. Thankfully, through learning, you can renew your passion for life as you discover many things that may interest you. Maybe what made you unhappy is that you found out too late that you took a degree program that you don't enjoy. This does not mean that you have to resign to failure and settle for a career in the field of that degree. By opening your heart to more opportunities to acquire knowledge in various other programs, you can get a chance to land a career in a field you enjoy. As a result, your life starts to feel enjoyable and meaningful to you.

☞ **It makes life more interesting and fun**: The world is vast and full of endless opportunities for adventure and growth. The more you learn, the more variety in your life. You can do many things instead of being stuck to the same old routine every day. If you see that you're unhappy with your job, learning can be your lifesaver. Through acquiring new skills, you will be able to start new ventures or move to a more friendly work environment you prefer. People who are learned tend to also be very interesting. They are articulate and often have many thought-provoking things to share. This works to your advantage socially. People gravitate more toward someone who can add value to their lives.

☞ **It can lead to radical career advancement**: The chances of getting promoted if you keep doing the same things that allowed you to be at the level you're at now are always slim to none. Growing in your career requires you to demonstrate new skills, desirable behavioral qualities, and virtues that you can only have if you allow yourself to learn new things. There is no limit to the number of things you can achieve if you continue to educate yourself. Opportunities start to widen for you, depending on how wide your skillset is.

☞ **It improves your social cohesion (connection)**: People learn various things at different places. You can learn about a new hobby where you get the chance to meet and interact with others. This gives you a chance to grow your social circle and learn social skills. Whether it's formal or informal education, chances are that you will get a chance to do it with others. The more you mingle with others, the more your social intelligence develops. You can also have theoretical lessons about how to build relationships, which results in better social cohesion. Education helps people become responsible citizens and blend well in their communities. It helps you to be a person of necessity by being able to contribute positively to the growth of society.

☞ **It makes you feel good and positive**: Learning opens your mind to new perspectives. Sometimes, you might be down and in the depths of despair because your plan A of getting your dreams to come true might not be working. However, learning can overturn those negative situations by introducing you to new suggestions of how you can go about things. This, in turn, makes you feel optimistic about life.

☞ **It builds strength of character, such as learning and endurance**: People who learn a lot tend to be wiser. Their approach to life shows prudence and thoughtfulness. When you are uneducated, it's easy to make poor choices in life or give up easily. However, education opens your mind and helps you be aware of the reality of what it takes to truly succeed. Success requires strength of character. Hence, learning can help you build helpful character traits that will enable you to win many battles in life. For example, when you learn through experience that resilience and endurance are the price you have to pay to win certain goals, you start to appreciate those attributes more.

☞ **It helps you manage your time effectively**: The more you learn, the more you realize that each day is packed with so many opportunities to make a difference in your life. This pushes you to become more disciplined so that you can harness those opportunities. When you learn about the value of time and life, it helps you come up with effective time management strategies that keep your life under control.

☞ **It makes you feel fulfilled with your life**: There are many problems you can avoid or solve if you only have the required information to excel. Continual learning helps to ensure that you stay mentally alert and full of wisdom. Life becomes more fulfilling and satisfying when we no longer have to do things in the same old, ineffective ways. Learning opens your eyes to better ways of living or doing things.

☞ **It helps your brain stay healthy**: Just like anything else that isn't put to good use eventually starts to rust or deteriorate, *not learning* also has a similar effect on the brain. Continual learning helps to keep the brain functioning at optimum levels. This, in turn, helps to slow down memory and cognitive strength decline. Especially as you grow older, your brain's functioning power starts to slow down, but you can slow this process by keeping your brain active through learning.

Even though the benefits of lifelong learning are obvious, there will still always be barriers hindering people from learning and unleashing their fullest potential. These barriers can include things like:

☞ Laziness

☞ Poor time management

☞ Lack of self-control

☞ Being negative

☞ Secluding yourself from others

☞ Being defensive when given constructive criticism

☞ Forgetfulness

☞ Little or no ambition. Being someone who just settles for less.

Develop a Curious Mind

Curiosity is an insistent hunger for answers, discovery, and novelty. To state it frankly, life can easily become boring when you stop watering your curiosity and applying yourself to new things. Being content is good. However, lacking curiosity means being too content with things in a rather dangerous way. The reason behind that is the fact that ignorance does not guarantee that you will be free from the consequences of being oblivious about important things you should have known.

Imagine settling for having the same meals every week even though there are more than a thousand recipes for making different meals. Wouldn't that rather be a tragedy? Imagine how much you would be missing out on! Food can be both satisfying and impactful on our health and well-being. This is just one example of how dire it is to lack curiosity. It puts you in a box and makes you recycle the same old patterns, even though you might be fed up with them.

Curiosity is the cure for boredom and mediocrity. Even Einstein used to credit his success with curiosity rather than intelligence. This is one of the most intelligent men who has ever walked on the face of this earth. If curiosity is what makes someone knowledgeable, then isn't it worth finding out how we too can be curious and use that to our advantage?

Below are ways you can employ to nourish your curiosity:

- ☞ **Become an avid, voracious reader:** Worried that you don't have enough funds to travel the world and learn new things? Don't worry, there is an alternative way you can still bring the world to your nearest proximity. That is through being a voracious wide reader. There might be topics you naturally gravitate toward; consider starting with those subjects to develop your reading habit. Once you're locked in that world, begin to explore other topics outside your scope of interest. You may be surprised to learn that something you never thought would interest you is captivating. Become a wide reader. Set monthly and annual goals for how many books you would love to read. If you're not much of a hard-copy book reader, opt for audiobooks and listen to podcasts. All these avenues allow you to know about a lot of things.

The more you realize how much you didn't know before, the more you will be motivated to keep having a curious mind that allows you to grow unceasingly.

☞ **Be curious about why people think the way they do:** Oftentimes, we pass judgment and shut down people who don't share the same perspectives we do. We may find them to be either weird or not so smart. But in hindsight, you will realize that just because others don't think the way you do doesn't make them any less intelligent than you are. Listening to people with a curious mind instead of just waiting to interject and share your opinions enables you to deeply discover the different ways people see the world. Being open and genuinely interested in understanding why they view things the way they do will help you learn so much. Remember, when you talk, you are likely to learn nothing. You will just be sharing what you already know. But when you listen, chances are that you will be able to learn new ideas and also correct any misunderstandings you may have had about many things.

☞ **Don't be afraid or reluctant to ask any questions:** Most people hold themselves back from learning new things because of the fear of being perceived as dumb. Whenever you feel like what you're about to ask is dumb or something that will make you feel embarrassed, ask yourself, "What's the worst that can happen?" Oftentimes, we exaggerate the consequences we imagine will occur if we ask questions. You will be surprised that people love helping or feel like they are being helpful in some way. Hence, start being more free-spirited and less worried about asking what you need to. Show your appreciation for what others know that you might not know. Remember, your ignorance about a certain topic doesn't define you in any way. It doesn't mean that just because you are clueless about what others are knowledgeable about, that you're now a dull person. Not at all. When this misconception is corrected, it frees you to explore the world with more autonomy and confidence. Ask questions! Whenever you don't ask something, the answer will always be no, or you will always be clueless about what's going on.

☞ **Build up your knowledge storeroom:** With the information age we are living in, it can be tempting to avoid memorizing important lessons and just rely on Google or AI technology. Beat the temptation to allow knowledge to only exist on a screen. That knowledge should also be stored in your brain. You won't always be in a position where you have to Google things to give answers. Be ready to face life by storing up your knowledge treasures in your mind. Improve your vocals by challenging yourself to learn at least one new word a day. Imagine how rich and fascinating your speech will become in just one month if you are determined to consistently learn just one new word a day!

☞ **Visit a library, bookstore, or any educational programs more often:** There are things in life that you won't know you love unless you give yourself the chance to explore. A library or bookstore gives you a wide range of choices to dive into and see what would pique your interest. You don't have to commit to anything too soon. All that's required of you to strengthen your curiosity muscles is to keep an open mind and browse through things. When something catches your eye, trust your intuition, and give it a chance. Explore what that thing is all about. Whether you grow to like it or not, you won't have any real loss because that experience would have added to your learning in some way. Either you learn what's for you or what's not for you.

☞ **Don't be defensive; allow others to teach you:** Teaching others is relatively easy, and it can be enjoyable for many reasons. It can make you feel smart and stroke your ego to some degree. It can make you feel like you're useful and contributing positively to other people's growth. However, it's important to remember that great teachers are also great learners. Allow yourself to be taught by others. When someone shows you your flaws, instead of lashing out or resenting them, choose to be curious as to why they feel that way about you. Genuinely wait for an answer from them. Listen carefully. This will help you become mindful of the impact of your actions or words when dealing with others. Once you have self-awareness, it gives you a chance to better yourself and correct what's wrong.

Lifelong Learning Strategies to Support Your Growth Mindset

We have already established that lifelong learning is being resolved by embracing ongoing self-taught life lessons. Adopting a growth mindset is at the core of this way of life. There is no limit to the number of activities you can embark on to facilitate this learning process. Let's now explore some suggested lifelong learning strategies that can help you foster a growth mindset:

☞ **Appreciate and accept that you already have what it takes to be a lifelong learner**: Our brains thrive when we continually feed them with useful information. This goes to show us that we are inherently designed to be lifelong learners. Even when you see how naturally curious children are, you can tell that's what we're all meant to be. Sadly, somewhere along the passage of time, people can start to become very close-minded and set in their ways, thereby stifling their ability to be more progressive learners. Once you recognize that you already have a curious mind that's thirsty for novelty, you can intentionally resurrect and activate it.

☞ **Set aside time for self-examination**: It's hard to have the motivation to do something when you believe that it won't make any difference. Find some time to reflect on yourself. Think about your life and all the things you have gone through up until now. Would you say your life reflects your true potential? Once you accept that there is so much more that you can accomplish if only you set your mind to it, your drive starts to rise. Become aware of all the fears and limitations holding you back from learning new things and creating a new reality for yourself. Once you have mindfulness about where you stand and where you can potentially be, nothing but your stand will stop you from moving forward.

☞ **Identify your fixed ways of thinking and replace them with a growth mindset**: There are things we become so comfortable with that we even fail to see how those things might be hindering us from growing. For example, let's say you get your dream job. After years of working that job, you realize that there are more opportunities for growing or even working remotely and having more control over your time. Your traditional mindset might scare you from taking the leap of faith and trying out the newly improved ways of doing your job. As a result, you might end up stuck in the 9-5 routine even though you have the chance to create a better quality of life. This is an example of someone who is set in their ways and averse to change. Hence, start taking note of all your fixed ways of doing things and questioning how you can adopt a growth mindset in those areas.

☞ **Embrace discomfort**: Charting new territory feels uncomfortable. Our brains love familiarity because it feels safe. Thus, be prepared for a mental battle where your mind will keep pulling you back to the old and making it hard for you to accept change. Discomfort doesn't mean that you're doing the wrong thing. Just accept that sometimes you might have to go through things you don't particularly like just so you can cross over to the greener side of things.

☞ **Carve out some time in your daily routine, specifically just for learning new things**: Learning doesn't always have to be rigid, serious, or daunting. It can be watching an interesting show that you never used to before. Or perhaps joining a social gathering that you wouldn't have ordinarily attended. Allow yourself to always have a set time each day for growing your knowledge and understanding of the world. It can even be just one hour. What matters is that you have to set aside a fixed time to do it, and then for the rest of the learning, you can do it anytime and anywhere as a way of life.

☞ **Learn through action**: Watching cooking or fashion videos can seem pretty informative. But you never actually know how much you have learned unless you put the knowledge into action. Start applying everything you learn as often as possible. It's only when you practically try things out that you will be able to know which knowledge you truly possess.

☞ **Celebrate growth, and don't wait for perfection**: You probably already have a vision of who you want to be. While that's very good, it's also important to be careful not to undermine who you are now and all the progress you make along the way. Don't be hard on yourself. Learn to fall in love each day with the level of wisdom you have at any given time. There is no end to learning, so you might as well enjoy the ride all the way!

☞ **Seek mentorship**: Working with advisors and mentors can greatly enrich your learning journey. Be open to continuous feedback for improvement. Working with others also helps you be accountable for your learning goals.

☞ **Remember that lifelong learning is a lifestyle, not a one-off activity to tick off**: By becoming a lifelong learner, you embrace growth opportunities as part of your everyday life. You expect to see them and embrace them with an open mind. Adopting lifelong learning as a lifestyle gives you a chance to always beat the older version of who you used to be. You become better and better with each passing day.

☞ **Believe that you can be a competent lifelong learner**: If you used to tell yourself that there are certain things you can never be good at, now is the time to stop talking that way once and for all. You cannot grow if you continue to hold on to limiting beliefs. Choose to be confident and trust that, through practice and repetition, there is no skill under the sun that's too hard for you to master.

☞ **Put yourself out there and explore new things**: There are things you can learn in the comfort of your home, but don't limit your learning to that environment alone. Be brave enough to step outside and explore what the great world has in store for you. Regularly try out things that you adore and take an interest in. Even if it's just briefly, what matters is that you keep yourself growing and don't get too stuck in your comfort zone.

☞ **Share your experiences**: It's exciting and encouraging to hear how others appreciate your new insights and wisdom. Don't be afraid to share what you learned with your loved ones or anyone willing to listen. Who knows, you can even start earning from sharing thoughts about your learning journey if you do something like post videos on social media. The more you share, the more you become aware of the difference your new knowledge makes to others.

☞ **Take advantage of the dynamic technology available to you**: Nowadays, it's so easy to learn so many things free of charge in the comfort of our own homes. You can use technology as a tool to continuously educate yourself. Rather than just mindlessly surfing social media, become intentional about how you use it so that it benefits you more profoundly.

☞ **Don't be afraid to make personal investments**: Some core lessons may require you to pay for a course or some form of training. Don't be afraid to invest in such opportunities whenever you can since you are guaranteed to have a solid learning experience. Even if you are already happy with your job, consider training for other skills so that you can become a ripe prospect for promotion. These investments can also help you create or be eligible for work opportunities that can provide additional streams of income.

☞ **Exercise**: At some point, you may get tired from learning. Don't be afraid to reward and pamper yourself with a break. Exercise and staying hydrated can also rejuvenate you physically and mentally. If you are having a marathon e-learning session, occasionally take time to do stretching exercises. Make sure that you learn in a balanced way so that learning doesn't end up making you burn out.

☞ **Create a "to learn" list**: Create a list of all you want to learn to help you streamline and organize your learning journey. Think about all the things you have always wanted to know how to do. Make a list of those things and set short- and long-term goals for when you would like each item to be ticked off. A list gives you a great sense of accomplishment once you manage to achieve the things there. It motivates you to even keep adding to that list.

Suggested Growth Mindset Activities to Enjoy

☞ **Introduce playful learning to your to-do list**: There are activities that are so empowering yet also fun to do. These include doing things like painting, drawing, playing puzzles, 30-second games, sudoku, dancing, and many other fun activities that grow your overall skills.

☞ **Set monthly goals**: Having a 30-day challenge can make it easier to review your progress in a short period. Thirty days doesn't seem like a hectic period of time to opt for. Make a list of all the habits you would like to try out in one month, and then review your progress daily or weekly. Make it fun by doing this challenge with friends who are also determined to grow with you.

☞ **Change your routine when necessary**: Just like in exercising, if you do the same sets of exercises every time, you eventually stop getting as many results as you could. When you hit this period, that's when you know that it's time to change the type of exercises you are doing to get the best results. Similarly, a certain routine can work for only a specific amount of time. As you get better and reach greater dimensions of who you are, it will be necessary to upgrade your routine and make it suit who you are now. You should also ensure that your routine always has time to do things you enjoy. This keeps it interesting and makes you look forward to successfully following through with your routine.

☞ **Always celebrate your success and other people's accomplishments**: It takes courage and tenacity to be a lifelong learner. Please always remember to reward yourself and appreciate each step of the way. Avoid comparing yourself with others, and always remember that you have to win your race. Being able to focus on your lane allows you to be secure and confident no matter what's going on outside of you. Become a cheerleader for other people's success and genuinely support them. The positive energy you share with others is likely to bounce right back at you.

Are you ready to be a lifelong learner? Can you already envision the exciting life full of novelty and endless possibilities that awaits you now? It's time to evolve! Let's now hop to the next chapter to learn about how the growth mindset is going to enrich your life.

Chapter "Good Will"

Helping others without expectation of anything in return has been proven to lead to increased happiness and satisfaction in life.

I would love to give you the chance to experience that same feeling during your reading or listening experience today...

All it takes is a few moments of your time to answer one simple question:

> **Would you make a difference in the life of someone you've never met—without spending any money or seeking recognition for your good will?**

If so, I have a small request for you.

If you've found value in your reading or listening experience today, I humbly ask that you take a brief moment right now to leave an honest review of this book. It won't cost you anything but 30 seconds of your time— just a few seconds to share your thoughts with others.

Your voice can go a long way in helping someone else find the same inspiration and knowledge that you have.

Are you familiar with leaving a review for an Audible, Kindle, or e-reader book? If so, it's simple:

If you're on **Audible**: just hit the three dots in the top right of your device, click rate & review, then leave a few sentences about the book along with your star rating.

If you're reading on **Kindle** or an e-reader, simply scroll to the last page of the book and swipe up—the review should prompt from there.

If you're on a **Paperback** or any other physical format of this book, you can find the book page on Amazon (or wherever you bought this) and leave your review right there.

Chapter 5

All the Gifts a Growth Mindset Brings

Life either becomes more fulfilling or troublesome, depending on the mindset you choose to adopt. The way people with a growth mindset and fixed mindset experience reality is completely polar opposites. For the person with a fixed mindset, their life experiences are likely to always be repetitive and have very little to no degree of novelty at all. This is because their way of thinking makes them hold on to the idea that their abilities will always be unchangeable. Envisioning themselves as being able to learn and master new skills and evolve to become a different person is extremely hard for them. On the other hand, the life of someone with a growth mindset is likely to be packed with vastly different experiences and a consistent record of continual improvements. They experience so much novelty and growth in almost all the areas of their lives, and this makes that kind of existence more thrilling and worth pursuing.

Is someone born with a fixed or growth mindset? If you think about it, all human beings are born with a growth mindset. If that were not so, then babies wouldn't be able to talk, crawl, walk, and learn all sorts of things as they grow. However, somewhere down the line, either one's environment or acquired fears start to stifle that growth mindset. This is when people begin to view themselves in very counterproductive ways and adopt limiting beliefs. Embracing labels and confining yourself to some title or version of a person society gave you started to become the norm.

It is at this point that the work of personal development has to be taken seriously for people to break free from the fixed mindset of being hammered in their psyche.

To give an analogy that demonstrates how people with a fixed and growth mindset operate, consider this story: A group of students from different faculties were asked to spend a day experiencing what their fellow students in other fields learned. Architecture students were sent to spend a day in the law faculty. While law students were directed to the architecture faculty, initially, when this exercise was introduced to them, none of the students knew what was going on and why they had to do that. It just came as an instruction that they would all be visiting those places, and all they had to do was learn as much as possible and see if they could grasp any new lessons in fields unfamiliar to them. Perhaps an expected good outcome would be law students learning how to design a basin plan for a particular building, or the other way around, architecture students learning something about law and order or how to handle a court case.

As the day passed, some observers noted remarkable differences in the attitudes that all the students had. Some of them seemed to approach that exercise with an open mind, distinct curiosity, and prolonged interest in what they were learning, even though it wasn't easy for them to grasp. On the other hand, others only managed to retain their concentration for a short fraction of time—they were already absentminded or seemed hopeless. When asked why they appeared disinterested, some of them shared that the faculty was just not their piece of cake, and they couldn't find themselves having any genuine interest in the subject, so they just chose to give up and wait to return to their core areas of interest. Others also shared that it was too hard and there was no point in trying.

Surprisingly, when students with a growth mindset were interviewed about why their interest seemed to linger much longer despite experiencing challenges with grasping what was being taught, they gave an inspiring answer. They shared that even though this wasn't familiar territory to them, they believed that through putting in more effort, being patient with themselves, and remaining with an open mind, they would eventually get the hang of things. Some even chuckled and smiled coyly as they mentioned that maybe they might even fall in love with the subject with time and be profoundly interested in it. At the end of the day, when the overall performance of the students was assessed, it was observed that students who exhibited a growth mindset learned more than 35% of the lessons that were delivered to them that day. On the other hand, those who showed signs of having a fixed mindset quickly burned out and performed very poorly. Most of them learned, on average, about 5 to 15% of what was taught after being tested.

When the objective of the experiment and results for all the students were announced, everyone was in awe of how powerful that experience was in helping them to understand themselves. It was clear that the secret to growth was undoubtedly being purposeful about having a growth mindset. On the other hand, failure becomes inevitable whenever you choose to close your mind and believe that you are only good at what you already know.

One can only imagine the extent of massive growth we all hold ourselves back from experiencing whenever we keep our mindsets fixed. This chapter will now give you a glimpse of the life you could create when you finally make up your mind to fully embrace the growth mindset at all times. If you've never felt immensely excited and in love with your life, chances are that once you take this leap of faith to have a growth mindset, you will never be the same! Only abundance and continuous improvement await you. That is indeed a life worth waking up to every day.

How a Growth Mindset Improves Your Education

When you look at your current level of intelligence and education, would you say you believe that where you are is where you should be? Would your education and skills level have significantly advanced if you had decided to be purposefully growth mindset oriented? Chances are that there is no doubt you would be very knowledgeable of way more things than you know now. And yes, this also includes those who may feel financially constrained to further their education. In the information age we are now living in, there are more doors for educational advancement open than you can ever imagine. Let's explore how a growth mindset can shift you to a whole new dimension education-wise.

Below are the Benefits of developing a growth mindset in your education:

- ☞ It fosters resilience and tenacity.

- ☞ It enables you to maintain focus and remain engaged in your pursuits.

- ☞ It creates a conducive and supportive learning environment.

- ☞ It helps you to improve your academic performance.

Strategies for Developing a Growth Mindset in Your Education

- ☞ Compliment and put more emphasis on effort than making the result the big deal.

- ☞ Invest in training your memory to be sharper.

- ☞ Embrace discomfort and water your curiosity to understand new things.

- ☞ Be patient when experiencing difficulties in mastering new things.

- ☞ Change your "I cant's" to "Not yet."

☞ Set short-, medium-, and long-term educational goals.

☞ Overcome the fear of asking for help.

☞ Keep an open mind for new opportunities.

How a Growth Mindset Improves Your Career

Benefits of developing a growth mindset in your career:

☞ You become more flexible and adaptable to change:

☞ Your problem-solving skills grow.

☞ You become a great team player.

☞ You face challenges with bravery and courage instead of resisting change.

☞ You learn many things and can easily get promoted.

Strategies for Developing a Growth Mindset for Career Advancement

☞ Practice active listening and don't interrupt others

☞ Don't be quick to shut down other people's ideas

☞ Try out different approaches to handling challenges

☞ Learn from mistakes and ask for performance feedback

☞ Put in effort to analyze and understand why things didn't go the way you expected them to (Failure)

☞ Stop running away from challenges

☞ Set learning goals and celebrate your small wins

☞ Observe others who are doing well

☞ Ask questions

☞ Become aware of what triggers you to use the fixed mindset as a defense mechanism

☞ Build good relationships and maintain a supportive network

Additional tips:

☞ **Encourage people to work together and resolve any differences as soon as possible:** When people are fighting, their instincts may be to avoid each other at all costs. When you also have a feud with someone, it can make you not want to work with them. Instead of canceling out people when they clash with you, try to put in the effort to build a positive relationship. Don't assume that just because people are not getting along, that's the end of the road. Be open to appreciating that when people see you put in effort to resolve things, they are likely to reciprocate and be willing to smooth things over too.

☞ **Praise the efforts of your teammates and keep challenging each other to grow:** People are generally used to putting more emphasis on the outcome of things. However, this stifles the growth mindset and prevents people from appreciating their efforts and growth process. Start to compliment your efforts and other people's too. Celebrate the process and remember that you're not only supposed to be proud of yourself at the end. The fact that you are putting in effort every day to move forward is worth your recognition. Once you start practicing appreciating all your efforts, it will inspire you to always be motivated to keep putting in more effort. Think of it this way: There is so much we all want to do for our loved ones, but if they choose not to appreciate what we have done for them so far, it discourages us from exploring more ways to make them happy. Hence, begin to feel proud of every effort you have put in so far. You deserve that acknowledgment and appreciation.

☞ **Track the progress of goals and be open to switching strategies when needed:** Setting goals is one thing, but following up on them to ensure that they are fulfilled is another. Once things start to seem like they are heading south, you might be tempted to give up on those goals and assume that failure is inevitable, just like in the past. Embracing the growth mindset means you now recognize how counterproductive that pattern is. Instead of acting in the same old, defeated ways, you chose to track your progress with a mindset of being open to putting into new mechanisms to increase the chances of success. Trying out new ways to achieve a goal means that you have to be open to possible failures. However, those should not be considered failures because it's a necessary trial-and-error process to find the best solutions. Start being persistent in going after your goals and never give up just because one approach you used didn't work.

☞ **Model the growth mindset first before expecting others to be on your team:** We've all experienced how frustrating it can be to repeatedly tell someone how to do the right thing, and they still choose otherwise. *Telling* someone something, no matter how right you are, will not always guarantee that they will listen to you. One of the best ways to move people into taking their rightful actions is to inspire them through your deeds. When you pioneer being a growth mindset-oriented person, it demonstrates to the whole team that they too, can do it. You can do this by showing your team that you aren't afraid to make mistakes, that you take criticism with grace, that you are willing to explore different perspectives, and that you have learning goals. If you consistently do this until you yield great results, your example will inspire everyone else to follow suit.

How a Growth Mindset Improves Your Relationships

Benefits of a growth mindset in your relationships:

☞ Your self-awareness grows, and you're likely to act more responsibly due to being open to changing things you do that could potentially destroy your relationships.

☞ You become a good listener.

☞ You give others a second chance when they wrong you.

☞ You don't hold on to grudges.

☞ You'll stop torturing yourself or others by expecting perfection all the time.

☞ Your communication becomes more effective and healthier.

☞ You experience a lot of adventures.

☞ You become more accommodating and open.

Strategies for Developing the Growth Mindset in Your Relationships

☞ Silence the inner critic: Everyone has a mean inner voice. Practice not listening to it and focus on edifying messages instead.

☞ Use positive affirmations for promoting growth: Negative thoughts are also affirmations. So, instead of forcing them on you, start to repeat positive words and statements to yourself.

☞ Be open to constructive criticism and use it to better yourself: When you perceive what others say as negative, you become defensive and fail to learn anything new. Start assuming the best whenever you receive feedback.

☞ Set targets for progressively overcoming your insecurities: You can't fix all your problems at once. Give yourself step-by-step targets for what you can focus on.

☞ Encourage others, and don't be quick to point out flaws: If you criticize and often disparage others, it disheartens them from trying again. The best way to make people do better is to encourage and acknowledge their efforts so far.

☞ Network continuously and reach out to existing friends to strengthen your social circle: There are so many friendships you can build as often as you want. Nowadays, you can even do so virtually. Start being intentional with the growth of your relationships. Make a vision together with your friends and family of how you would like your relationship to grow, and then work on it together.

☞ Try out new things with the people in your life: The growth mindset is all about being open to change and continuous learning. Set daily targets for new things you would like to try out.

Interactive Activities to Promote the Growth Mindset

Setting monthly goals is a good place to start when escaping a fixed mindset. To get you used to ditching your comfort zone, consider trying out any of these activities if you haven't yet:

- ☞ Research and try out at least one passive income-generating opportunity every month.

- ☞ Try out new hobbies like sunrise or sunset photography, drone racing, joining a book club, becoming an influencer, solving puzzles, or learning a musical instrument.

- ☞ Set a goal for how many new friends you would like to have every month. Alternatively, you can set a goal for all the dying relationships in your life that you would like to resurrect.

- ☞ Learn at least one musical instrument.

- ☞ Travel somewhere new at least once a month.

- ☞ Revolutionize your closet by changing or upgrading your existing primary fashion.

- ☞ Learning a new course and applying for a new occupation is an unfamiliar field.

- ☞ Start showing affection to the people in your life in unpredictable and new ways.

- ☞ Forgive everyone who has hurt you, including yourself.

☞ Start ending every negative sentence you say with a positive. For instance, you can say, "Today I wasn't very productive, but I can still make the most of the three hours left before midnight."

☞ Revise your vision and dream bigger.

There is no doubt that a life lived with a growth mindset is the ultimate solution to most, if not all, of the problems we face. Start writing a blueprint or vision board of how you would love your life to now transform as you purposefully apply the growth mindset. Everything you have ever dreamed of is possible to achieve. Through the growth mindset, allow yourself to finally let go of all your limitations. You have infinite potential for unstoppable growth. It's time to use that potential and make it count.

Chapter 6

The Role of Habits and Mindfulness

Does life ever feel like you are constantly reliving your past, even though you desperately don't want to? Why do people's past experiences and versions of who they used to be keep surfacing in the present? Even though life may have significantly changed with time, you might still notice patterns of undesirable habits or paradigms that keep you stifled and unable to fully make the most of your present reality and enjoy it.

Just having the intention of not letting the past control you won't guarantee that it will stop surfacing. Wishing that you won't struggle with the same things that hold you back won't stop your fears and habits from holding you back either. The solution to breaking free from past limitations lies in embracing mindfulness and purposefully doing things that reinforce the new version of yourself you want to become.

Consider this example: An avoidance attachment style is more likely to develop in someone who experienced caregiver neglect as a child. Even though they crave intimacy, they might still avoid it out of fear that their loved ones will disappear and leave them alone again. As a result, when they grow into adults, their biggest desire is to be loved and have intimate connections. But even though that's what they want, they would still most likely repel that love and intimacy by avoiding it when it shows up out of fear that it will all end, and they will be hurt again. As a result, their lives become a vicious cycle of always craving love but pushing it away even though doing so hurts them.

Unless someone like this is mindful of what's going on and why they act the way they do, they are likely to continually self-sabotage and destroy their opportunities to build meaningful relationships. Self-awareness becomes the key that will unlock their breakthrough, as having a thorough understanding of what's going on will empower them to change.

There are many ways to achieve mindfulness. One of the most effective strategies is to have what's called "Inner Space Therapy" (IST). This technique allows you to have interactive exercises that help you unearth underlying thoughts and core beliefs that govern your actions. It helps with self-discovery and mindfully dealing with your past. Through this sort of therapy, you can develop a deep awareness of your behavioral patterns, emotional ecosystem, and paradigms. Your past trauma can control you so much that almost every decision you make is governed and influenced by your fears and limiting beliefs derived from past wounds. When taking this form of therapy, you become very conscious of energy, yourself, others, and how to manifest the reality you wish to see.

When it comes to breaking free from your old self, choosing new habits, and sticking to them goes a long way toward fostering true transformation. Instead of worrying about all the wrong things that you need to stop, it's better to focus on all the new habits you would like to adopt. By doing so, naturally, the old habits phase off.

Let's review some of the new habits you can start practicing:

- ☞ Waking up early consistently

- ☞ Eating healthy meals and saying no to eating too late

- ☞ Exercise at least three times a week

- ☞ Drinking lots of water even when you don't feel like doing it

- ☞ Planning your next day (like the night before, so that you don't waste time doing aimless things)

- ☞ Not saying anything when you're angry.

- ☞ Having at least 6–8 hours of good sleep every night

- ☞ Making a vision board and sticking to your life goals

- ☞ Giving your full attention when someone speaks to you (avoiding looking distracted or using the phone)

☞ Learning new languages or cultures

☞ Practicing a good skincare routine every day.

☞ Warming up your stomach with a glass of warm lemon water, especially the first thing before you eat

☞ Let go of old things you no longer need and donate them to people who need them the most

☞ Learn new recipes and try at least three of them a week

☞ Never gossip or grumble; treat everyone the way you would want them to treat you

☞ Take yourself out and prioritize your self-care

☞ Learn new ways to articulate yourself clearly and effectively

☞ Repeat positive affirmations during your meditation time

☞ Say or do at least one thing that shows your loved ones your affection for them

☞ Creating a culture of celebrating small wins

☞ Never leave your room without making your bed and tidying up

☞ Focus very well during work time and have regular downtime

☞ Do one thing you enjoy each day

☞ Network regularly to make new friends

☞ Upgrade your wardrobe and dress in a stylish way

☞ Cultivate a mindset and attitude of gratitude

☞ Smile more

☞ Forgive yourself, let go of the past, and focus on the now

☞ Save and invest some of your income

☞ Beat the impulse to respond instantly to all messages that come your way; take control of your time

These are just a few examples of positive habits you can practice. However, mastering new habits is not always easy. Sometimes, people relapse into their old ways. To ensure that this doesn't happen to you, let's now study the art of habit formation.

How to Establish a Habit

Habit formation impacts how your brain functions. The habits you are accustomed to now have formed their neural pathways in your brain. This means that they are now part of who you are. Starting a new habit means creating new neural pathways that will become a part of your reinvented self. To ensure that this brain development process is successful, your steps in fostering new habits have to be incremental. When you attempt to do very hard things that you didn't warm up your brain to, chances are that your body and mind will resist those changes greatly, and that is why you see many people regressing to their old ways.

Let's get started with steps that can help you successfully create and sustain new habits:

Step 1: Choose to focus on only one new habit at a time: When you are super motivated and determined to make changes, the courage to try out many new habits at the same time will be relatively high. However, doing that seldom works in the long run because of a concept known as "ego depletion." This refers to the phenomenon where you won't have enough willpower to do many things at the same time. Ego depletion is an obstacle to habit formation because, as much as you want to make changes, your mind and body may not be ready for all that yet. For this reason, it's important to get your willpower to grow by pacing yourself using one habit at a time. That way, you can focus on directing your willpower toward getting that one habit you selected checked off soon. Thus, once you are ready to make changes, first learn a lot about the new habit you would like to try out. Research the different ways you can do it and select the most fun way for you. For example, if you want to have abs, doing sit-ups is helpful, but it may not be your cup of tea. However, that shouldn't be a problem at all because there are many other exercises you can try out to achieve the same results, such as bicycle crunches, running, plank exercises, and so forth.

Step 2: Have at least 30 days of committed dedication to consistently doing that new habit: In general, it takes about 21 days to build a habit if you are consistent. However, some people may take longer than that. That amount of time gives the brain enough time to form new neural pathways, which enable the new habit to become an ingrained part of who you are. During this phase, focus all your attention and energy on successfully making that habit every day. You will feel tired and want to quit. However, remember that that's just your body not getting used to the new you. If you persevere, things will take a positive turn soon.

Step 3: Create a routine: This will anchor the new habit. When habits are based on feelings and motivation alone, they easily fade away. You need something more solid than that. Create a routine where you can have a specific time and place when you will practice your new habit. Your routine shouldn't be too complicated; it should mainly encompass the main things you do daily. Try your best to ensure that you have an environment that will give you the least resistance to your habit.

Step 4: Start with small habits: Since it takes time for the brain to get used to big habits, starting small is always a win-win situation. Focus on making consistent, small changes that aren't too time-consuming. For example, if you used to rarely have any green in most of your meals, you can start adding a salad to every meal. If there are calls you have been postponing, you can start making at least one call a day to resurrect your relationships, one step at a time. This might seem trivial, but surprisingly, this is how transformation takes place successfully.

Step 5: Don't give up or skip a day: Skipping one day may seem like it's not a big deal, but in reality, it is. What's happening is that doing so confuses the mind. It's like trying out a new skin product, and then before the weekends, you start applying a different one simply because you feel like you aren't seeing the difference or think it won't matter. Doing that slows down the healing and restoration of your skin and can even cause you to experience an adverse reaction like having a rush or burning your skin. Similarly, even if you aren't in the mood, always exercise your willpower to stick to the process. You will have valid reasons for skipping some days; try your best not to give in to those excuses, at least for those first thirty days you committed to.

Step 6: Prepare for challenges: Everything worth having usually comes at a prize. With habit formation, there are obstacles you are bound to face at one point or the other. These may include not having adequate time, oversleeping, fatigue, a lack of motivation, being too emotionally unstable to get things done, and many other unforeseen problems. To counter such situations, you can employ the "If then" mindset to better respond to challenges. For example, when your car doesn't have enough gas for you to go to the gym, you can say, "If my car doesn't have enough gas by the time I need to head out to the gym, I will just work out at home instead." Or if you oversleep, you can say, "If I oversleep and miss my morning meditation time, I will forego my nap time and use it to meditate instead. This way of thinking helps you to proactively plan for any challenges and not be swayed by them.

Step 7: Monitor and proclaim to others about your new habit: When you track how well you are committing to your plans, it keeps you focused. Moreover, when you share with others about your journey, it gives you a greater sense of responsibility and encourages you to be accountable for your words. You are more likely to stick to your plan because you know that others are watching and rooting for you. To help you track your habits successfully, you can join a community and share your progress with others or have an individual accountability partner. Or you can use phone reminders that will keep you aware of your progress and the next session for implementing your habit.

Step 8: Appreciate and celebrate crucial milestones: Being able to successfully carry out your habit for a week without fail is a huge achievement to not sideline. You deserve to take a moment and reward yourself for that progress! Don't wait until you are done completing the whole thirty days before you decide to reward yourself. The process of habit formation doesn't have to always feel gruesome or boring. You can celebrate your milestones by enjoying a cozy evening with your loved ones while playing games or having a family bonding session. You could buy yourself somewhere or just celebrate in any way you would enjoy. Having fun during the process should be one of your core values!

Step 9: Reinvent yourself: The last step of the process is to get comfortable with your new identity. Let that habit be part of your new identity and continuously stick to it so that it can be reinforced in you. Let's say you didn't know how to cook, and for those thirty days, you learned so many recipes and upgraded your cooking skills. Now, your vocabulary has to change. Instead of saying I am not a good cook, start talking differently and say, "I am such a great cook." Proudly and confidently embrace that new identity. Are you now ready to start that habit you've always wanted to have?

Waiting for the right time to start a new habit will delay you from getting anything done. Chances are that you will never feel like making the habit of the time. This is why being decisive and resilient matters. Starting new habits is based on the choices you make. Sticking to them also depends on your choices. Never forget to start your habits using these simple steps. As you continue to practice your habits, sooner than you imagined, you will be able to execute your new habits seamlessly or on autopilot!

How to Use Mindfulness to Support Your Growth Mindset

Mindfulness is the art of being self-aware of all sides of yourself. It's appreciating that, as much as you want to achieve the best for yourself, there will be times when you will fail or feel demotivated to take action. It's hard to have a growth mindset if you don't feel safe being that way. Embracing the growth mindset means that you are conscious that you will have to go through times of learning without any clue of what you're making and that's okay. Without mindfulness, a growth mindset can start to feel torturous or even impossible to accept because you start to become too hard on yourself when things aren't working out as well as you wish them to. This is why using mindfulness to support your growth mindset will help you to always keep moving forward despite having issues along the way. You become mindful that every obstacle you face is part of what's necessary for you to come off victorious on the other side. Mindfulness helps you to not be judgmental and harsh towards yourself and others. It creates a safe space for growth and self-compassion.

Through mindfulness, you can focus on celebrating the process of getting where you want to go instead of only being kind to yourself when you attain the outcome you want.

Mindfulness also gives you room to feel your emotions and process them when you're ready to. It encourages you to purposefully focus on what's going right instead of ruminating on things you think aren't going well. Through it, you can foster gratitude and create a joyful atmosphere for growing. You can actively pay attention to what matters whenever you are mindful of what's important.

You can practice mindfulness to support having a growth mindset by:

☞ Take some time to listen to your thoughts and process them every day.

☞ Silence any negative self-talk or walk away from bad energy.

☞ Not judging or pressuring yourself.

☞ Writing down your feelings and practicing what to say before having difficult conversations.

☞ Whenever you feel anxious, always take a moment to breathe deeply before saying anything.

☞ Be purposeful with your actions and choice of words.

☞ Doing cognitive-behavioral therapy (using new actions to break free from old, limiting habits and beliefs).

☞ Having inspirational quotes that remind you about your core values and vision.

Now is the time when you have to put into action what we have learned so far. Even though you may feel ill-prepared, remember that what matters is taking action; that's what makes a difference.

Interactive Exercise

Breathing exercises are one of the best ways to promote mindfulness and learn to be fully present in your body and the now. To train your mind to be focused and not have your thoughts pulled away in all sorts of directions, consider doing these mindfulness exercises:

☞ **Mindful observing**: Start observing how people react to your energy. Focus on grasping every micro-expression and decoding their body language. Doing this will help you pick up patterns of what makes people respond to you positively and what makes them react negatively to you.

☞ **Mindful awareness**: This is when you give your full attention to everything you are doing. When your thoughts are focused on the task at hand, you are more likely to perform very well on those tasks. This is very similar to mindful immersion when you fully engage in what you're doing.

☞ **Mindful listening**: Start not only listening with your ears but also listening with your heart. Suspend any preconceptions you may have when listening to people. Just allow yourself to fully and freshly absorb what they are sharing. This will make people feel truly seen and heard.

☞ **Mindful gratitude**: This is when you purposefully cultivate a culture of appreciating many things in your life. Instead of focusing on what you don't have, start expressing your gratitude more for what you have. This invites more abundance into your life.

These new habits can open the door to that new life with greater success and contentment that you have been dearly longing for. Remember to always rely on your willpower and choices to make progress. To succeed in habit formation, your feelings always have to be trained to submit to your willpower and commitments.

Chapter 7

Setting Goals and Seeing Personal Growth

Going with the flow and just randomly living out each day without any clear plans can be very tempting. It's less pressure on you and less responsibility, right? Wrong! Not planning your days is an undisputed recipe for disaster. You lose so much time and miss out on opportunities to make meaningful progress in your life. This is why goal setting is a fundamental principle of success that everyone embracing a growth mindset needs to centralize in their lives. When you set and achieve goals, you become less stressed about unfulfilled dreams because each day becomes a chance to make them come true.

Consider the stories of the goal-setting giants we are about to review who managed to achieve tremendous success because they were intentional about it (Stunning Motivation, 2020). They envisioned their lives—who they wanted to be, what they wanted to achieve, and when. They wrote down those plans, mapped them, and then set to work to make things happen.

Tony Robbins is a tremendously successful life coach who has touched the hearts of many people across the world. His skills, love for people, and expertise helped him change their lives. In one of his best-selling books, *Awaken the Giant With,* he shared his story about how his success was mapped long before everything manifested. He set very clear and specific goals, which were time-bound. They encompassed everything he wanted to achieve and be. His goals also included the things he no longer wanted to settle for. He confronted his limiting beliefs and drafted his vision in a journal while sitting on the beach. Twenty years was the allotted time he gave himself to achieve all those goals. Six months down the line, he refined his goals and specified what he wanted to achieve in less than a decade.

He also detailed the actions and steps he would have to faithfully take to manifest the success he envisioned. Imagine specifying exactly the kind of woman you would want to marry and then being able to attract and marry that exact person. This was Tony's reality. Just a year later, after setting those specific goals, he was already being interviewed about his success and how he was able to do so much. And guess who he credited all that success to? Effective goal-setting. He wrote all his goals on an old Russian map. See the power of scripting?

Jack Canfield is another great example of someone who effectively set goals and was able to yield incredible results. Making your first million is the toughest thing. Once you do make it, things only get easier. Jack Canfield described how he was able to make his first million through the power of relentless goal-setting. He is an author, entrepreneur, and motivational speaker, among many other things. He wrote a best-selling book called *The Success Series.* He shared some of the things he did in his goal-setting journey. This included giving himself a target of making $100,000 in a year and then tapping it on his ceiling directly above his bed to ensure that he would see it every day. He would visualize what his lifestyle would be like once he started earning $100,000. He certainly was a lover of the lake house, so that too, wasn't left out of his vision. Once his goals were set, he shared that in about 30 days, he already had vast ideas of how he could attain $100,000.

Surprisingly, in less than a year, he was able to earn $92,000. This was indeed a groundbreaking financial achievement. This helped him and his wife's confidence to be reinforced, and she asked him if they could reach out for a million dollars this time. He reasoned that if it worked for $100,000, why shouldn't there be a good reason why they shouldn't try this exciting goal, too? Can you guess what they did next? They placed a million-dollar bill on the ceiling and placed it again directly over their bed on the ceiling. They set to work, and in just a few years, that first million dollars flooded in! He got a million-dollar check from the income he got through royalties for one of his best-selling books, *The First Chicken Soup for the Soul.* It is clear from this example that small thoughts and goals beget small ideas and progress. Conversely, big goals give birth to great ideas and inspire action in the right direction.

Bruce Less is a successful movie star and martial arts icon. His success was not by chance at all. He wrote himself a letter that described all the things he wanted to achieve. This included being an exciting performer, having financial abundance, and having world fame. Rightfully so, he achieved so many things in his letter to himself. Sadly, due to his death, some of the things he wanted to achieve weren't able to materialize. However, there is no doubt that the famous and loved philosopher and superstar was very intentional about his goals and did extremely well as a result.

The moral of all these inspirational stories is that, without solid intention and commitment to working towards your goals, no one can ever unleash their true potential to the fullest. When climbing up a mountain, you have to be purposeful about it. There is no way you can just wake yourself up. However, going downhill is way easier because there is less resistance. Through the inspiration of these stories, let's now dive deep into exploring crucial facets of goal setting and how you can start setting and achieving yours.

How to Set and Achieve Ambitious Goals

Goals are the plans you make for achieving any specific life dream or target you have. They bring so much joy after people fulfill them and also encourage you to grow and face your fears.

On a general level, people have five core needs such as those described by Maslow's hierarchy of pyramids. These include:

☞ Physiological needs: Such as water, good, and rest.

☞ Safety needs: Such as job security and a home.

☞ Love: Such as relationships that give us a sense of belonging.

☞ Esteem needs: Such as being respected, having significance, and a good status.

☞ Self-actualization: Such is knowing that you are working towards achieving your full potential.

When setting goals, you have to ensure that not just one of these categories is met but all 5. Pain and suffering usually come when our other fundamental human needs are ignored. Therefore, your vision board has to include plans about how you will achieve different goals in all aspects of your life and have balanced success.

Things that are your *needs,* such as what we described above, should always take precedence over things that are your *wants.* Your wants are usually the extrinsic things you desire but can live without, such as traveling to many countries, being famous, getting promoted, owning the coolest car, and so on. In the hierarchy of importance, these fall right below your needs and should never be the focus before your needs are met.

Now, let's unpack the process of goal setting. Below are the steps you can take to guide you:

1. **Set the intention**: The first step is to set the intention by deliberately choosing to think about goals and taking action. Psychologically, prepare

yourself by making up your mind to finally set goals and get things done. This is the decision-making stage; for this, you need to exercise your willpower to be firm and serious about goal-setting.

2. **Design your goals by scripting them**: Next, find a supportive environment where you can concentrate and be in touch with yourself. Think about what matters to you and what you would love to achieve without restraining yourself. Grab a journal and start writing down your vision. This is the broad blueprint for the outcome you want to see. After writing that big plan, start breaking it down into actionable steps or targets that you can do one at a time. This could be breaking down your master plan into what you will achieve in a week, month, year, or decade. In your plan, don't forget to write the reason why you want to achieve all those goals.

3. **Decipher what you need and the process of how you will take action daily**: Once your dream is well crafted. Now, critically think about all the resources you will need to achieve your goals. Decide on which process will work best for you. This could be drafting a specific routine and time-blocking your goals. Assemble as many resources as you can. It's most likely that the most important resource you will need is time. Part of planning a successful process for setting goals is also thinking about how you will manage your time effectively. Start reaching out for opportunities that will help

you get the rest of the resources you need to achieve your goals.

4. **Fight and overcome obstacles and limiting factors**: For every battle you go into, you are bound to face a foe. A successful goal-setter is someone who anticipates the enemy. You push ahead with what you will do when challenges come so that they don't take you by surprise and get you off course. At this stage, asking for help and enlisting other people's advice and feedback can help you overcome problems you will face along the way. Self-care should be prioritized at this stage because, without it, you may not be physically or mentally strong enough to show up for your goals.

5. **Stay in your lane and endure**: There will come many things that may tempt you to veer in the wrong direction. Some of these things can even be unavoidable problems, such as the loss of a loved one or illness. If such things happen, make a backup plan for how you will catch up and keep running your race. Focus on your goals and avoid allowing others to steal your attention and time from focusing on your lane. You will get tired, frustrated, and even hopeless at some points. But remember, the night only endures for a little while. Remain committed to your goals and keep going; this is the art of endurance.

6. **Celebrate your milestones**: As you keep working toward your goals every day, you will notice that your life will also start to change and reflect your

new mindset and focus. You will experience small and big wins along the way. Don't wait for your entire vision to be fulfilled before you give yourself permission to celebrate and appreciate your milestones.

This should become your lifestyle. You will notice that when you get into the habit of dreaming big and taking consistent steps to make those dreams a reality, your success becomes inevitable. Don't worry too much about the outcome. Just focus on winning every battle you face, one day at a time. Ensure that all your goals are realistic, time-bound, specific, and attainable. They should also be measurable goals where you can evaluate your progress regularly. To remember the key principles of goal-setting, consider memorizing this term:

> *SMART goals stand for specific, measurable, attainable, realistic, and time-bound goals. The stories you read at the beginning of this chapter are excellent examples of how to set SMART Goals.*

How to Track Your Progress and Adjust Goals When Necessary

The process of goal-setting itself can be very exciting. It makes us feel great just to think about all the things we want. But what matters most is also paying attention to how things are progressing once you start putting into action your goals. You can measure your goals through:

☞ Having clarity about exactly what you want to achieve. Don't just think about it; write it down.

☞ Decide when you want to achieve each specific goal. Time matters. Without a deadline, you risk wasting lots of time.

☞ The focus shouldn't just be achieving the grand plan. Set milestones that you can focus on in the short, medium, and long term.

☞ Keep records of your daily, weekly, monthly, and annual results. Use those reports to review what worked and what needs to be improved. Make room for feedback and adjust things when necessary.

Remember that things won't always go the way you expect them to. That doesn't mean you are failing! So, beware of being too hard on yourself. Once you review your goals, you can adjust them by organizing things according to the ones that matter the most. What you thought was going to be the most urgent and important goal is not always going to be what matters all the time. Thus, remember to be flexible to change and fluid where need be. Sometimes, you may also need to adjust your timeliness or the size of your goals. Allow yourself to have a trial-and-error stage before you are set in stone about the systems and things you will stick to. Continue to be open to constructive feedback and reflection.

Here are some pointers that can help you to stay in lane:

- ☞ Keep an open mind; sometimes, life will hand you opportunities that weren't part of your core plan. It's okay to grab them and slot them into your vision as well.

- ☞ Ditch negative self-talk and overthinking. Action is what will yield you continuous results. When tempted to just think and think and think... pause. Become clear about your action steps again and get back to work.

- ☞ Use your past successes as motivation to keep moving forward. Always remember why you are doing what you set your mind to. This will help you get through days when you won't be in the mood to put in the work.

- ☞ You can plan for additional challenges by enlisting the help of a coach or mentor. Or you can invest in learning new skills that will increase your ability to withstand adversity and any potential problems you may face.

Interactive Exercise

Before any big game, players always warm up to prepare their bodies and minds for the intense game awaiting them. Likewise, you too will certainly need a little warming up to get you ready for the implementation of your actual life goals and plans. This exercise will help you practice effective goal setting. Get ready to warm yourself up through this exercise:

1. Set aside time for this exercise. You will need at least two uninterrupted hours.

2. Next, direct your thoughts and focus on the present moment. You can find a cozy and comfortable place to sit as you do this.

3. Thereafter, start reflecting on your professional and personal life. What do you feel about where your life stands so far? Try to rate how happy you are about your work, relationships, health, social life, education, and skills. Think about how you have managed and run your life up until now. How well do you think your routine and schedule are working for you? This process of life examination is crucial to helping you become clear about your "Why?" Why should I do this? Through the results you will gather from this reflection exercise, you will know why it's important for you to make changes.

4. Next, get more specific and reflect on what worked in your professional and personal lives last year. Also, think about what didn't work and the reasons why. What could you have done better to get a different outcome?

5. Now, start to plan for the following year (assuming you do this exercise toward the year's end). Include clear plans about what sort of activities, business initiatives, relationships, and other goals you would

like to achieve in that way. Also, think about the process. How will you achieve those goals? Perhaps you will have to start being more assertive and kind to yourself, delegate some of your responsibilities, or reach out for new opportunities. Think about how you can achieve those goals less harshly or strenuously because setting unrealistic goals can make you give up along the way.

6. Write a list of all the possible roadblocks and issues you may face as you try to achieve your plans. Start preparing ahead of time for any unforeseen challenges. Is there anything that needs to be resolved before you unroll your plan? When are you going to get it sorted out as soon as possible? Think about the automated systems, tools, and apps you can use to make the process much easier for you to handle. For example, you could download apps that can help you have customized workout plans and recipes for your exercise goals or meal plans, respectively. Even plan for how you will reward yourself along the way.

7. Next, remember to pace yourself. Slow but sure wins the race. Starting with too much intensity without being rooted enough to maintain it, in the long run, can lead to imminent failure. Start with baby steps and gradually upgrade your amount of work with time. Focus on bringing your vision to fruition, and don't be distracted by looking at other people's lives. Negative comparison is one of the reasons why people can be so unhappy with

themselves even though they are already doing very well. Lastly, remember to set and maintain clear boundaries so that you always have the mental fortitude and room to prioritize what matters to you. When will you start? I hope soon!

Are you ready to get started with clarifying your vision and setting life-changing goals to make your dreams a reality? I believe you are. People who set goals and succeed at achieving them practice being disciplined individuals. It takes self-control, determination, self-belief, and courage to stay committed to manifesting the life you desire. Once you achieve your goals, you will notice that your desire to make a difference in many other people's lives will grow. Let's now review how you can create a life of greater significance and virtue by impacting the lives of others.

Chapter 8

Beyond Success—Contribution and Impact

Having a growth mindset is one sure way to manage your life effectively. You are guaranteed to experience continuous growth and success because your learning never reaches a limit. Every day is a chance to blossom further into something greater than what you've known. When your life is filled with so much abundance and positive changes, happiness becomes the by-product of having that continuous learning mindset. However, when the people around you don't think in this way and rather embody the fixed mindset, they can either slow you down or make you unhappy because of the polar opposite way of handling life that they tend to incline to. For example, if you are in a relationship with someone who always wants things to remain the same and gets defensive every time you give them constructive feedback about how to improve things, that relationship eventually starts to drain and impede your progress. This is why only having a growth mindset as an individual is good, but what's even better and far more important is also learning to inspire that way of thinking in others.

It may seem like having a growth mindset shouldn't be that difficult at all. But in reality, we know that it may be quite hard to foster it in people sometimes. This is because people have "fixed mindset triggers." When people perceive your feedback as a threat or criticism, they can easily lose touch with the real intention of your message and fall into a pattern of chronic defensiveness, shutting down, or being insecure. This hinders effective communication and inhibits progress. You end up circling in the same place with the same issues, be it at work, family, or in your intimate relationships and friendships.

Sometimes it can also be hard to foster a growth mindset at work due to the culture that people have practiced there for ages. If change is seldom welcomed or seen as a form of rebellion or a negative thing, then work can also start to be a place that's stifling you from unleashing your full potential.

If someone is always worried about looking smart and concerned with what others think of them, this slows them down from learning. Embracing the growth mindset means that you have to be willing to look like a fool sometimes, to be laughed at, and to face temporary defeat. Learning should be what matters to you more than being perceived as always right or smart.

Let's review a few examples of how you can successfully apply a growth mindset in different areas of your life so that not only you experience growth but other people in your life too.

The first example is in your intimate relationship. Every great relationship that is fulfilling always has growth in it. If things are always the same, both partners are likely to feel suffocated by the relationship. They can even start to look at other couples and envy how they are always growing closer and achieving so many new things together in life. For every relationship, there should always be things that the couple loves about each other that should remain consistently present. For example, if your partner fell in love with you because they enjoyed how chivalrous, kind, expressive, protective, caring, fun, and consistently communicative you were, then those things should always be there. Whenever you stop being that way, it can start to make the other person feel less attracted to you and dissatisfied with the relationship.

Even though the reasons why someone fell in love with you may still be there, it's not always guaranteed that being that way alone is what will keep your relationship strong throughout the years ahead. People start to grow, love, and expect new things. If you don't grow with them and remain stuck in the same pattern, your partner may begin to feel like they are outgrowing the relationship and need to be with someone more willing to embrace growth and development. Hence, if you are the one who has a growth mindset in the relationship, you have to be able to find effective ways to get your partner to be on board with you in the pursuit of continuous learning.

Find a way to help your partner understand how much you appreciate what they have already been contributing to the relationship. Next, inspire them to envision how your relationship can grow beyond what it currently looks like and think about what it will take for you as a couple to materialize that vision. If you've always loved how you spend time with each other, could there possibly be other ways of spending time together that you would love even more? Promote curiosity and ensure that your partner doesn't see your growth mindset talk as a form of criticism for how things are. Couples that create a safe space for growing together and reassure each other how much they will always be there for the relationship do great. Reminding your partner that even if you face failure in the process of trying new things, you will always have each other's back makes them more likely to have successful relationships and lasting marriages. A growth mindset keeps the spark and butterflies present in every romantic relationship. Spontaneity and novelty are encouraged, and this keeps your partner always intrigued and captivated by your journey together. However, with a fixed mindset, boredom and discontentment are likely to eventually strain the relationship because human beings are filled with positive growth and change.

The second example where you can promote a growth mindset is in your career or workplace. Have you ever wondered why many people tend to look for new jobs? Someone may love their job, but a few months down the line, they start to complain about many things and show great dissatisfaction. Why is this so? It's because progress makes people happy. No one is always going to be happy being in the same spot for too long. Promotions and career advancement make people more committed to their organizations or the companies they work for. If you are a leader or part of any team at work, think about how you can inspire your team to grow and create a fun work environment.

A great way that many successful leaders use to encourage a growth mindset at work is to create a culture that promotes mutual learning and discussions. Instead of just telling people what to do, involve them in the decision-making process. Challenge people to brainstorm new ideas and set up reward systems for promoting co-workers who try new things and contribute growth to the organization. Increase competence by encouraging people to research solutions instead of shying away from new opportunities because no one knows how to get things done yet. You can also promote a growth mindset by providing educational training sessions for people as often as possible. When your workforce is continuously unskilled, there is no limit to the number of things they can do. This also saves you from having to hire new staff all the time because you will be able to grow talent from within the pool of human resources you already have. During team meetings, encourage others to share their ideas. Don't allow one person to dominate and monopolize the entire discussion. This helps people to always learn from each other and experience growth.

In the last example, a crucial place you can promote a growth mindset is with your family and friends. Sometimes, the people we love can become the same people who prevent us from growing in our own lives. When you always swoop in to save others from facing challenges, it hinders them from being able to have a healthy dependence on others. Our families and friends can feel entitled to receive our help just because they are related to us in that way. If you enable them to have unhealthy expectations of you. They will continue to demand more until you are unable to look after yourself well because you are too busy taking responsibility for others.

Think about it this way: There were times when you didn't know how to win certain battles in your life, but you found a way. People didn't always come to your rescue and fight your battles for you. Why is it then that you think it's okay to fight everyone's battle and deny them the opportunity to experience the growth you did by figuring out ways to survive and thrive? In the same way you grew and learned new things, they will also grow and learn new things if you dare to stand your ground. You have to be able to set healthy boundaries with your loved ones and encourage them to unlock their potential. Things won't always be easy when you do this. They might be mad at you for not doing things for them. Even call you selfish. But that shouldn't get to your head. Give them space to grow and reinforce their strengths by reminding them how capable they are. You can show them the way, but don't walk the road for them. This is true love. Wouldn't it be beautiful to see your family and friends all grown and able to do new things for themselves, just like you did? If you can overcome the fixed mindset, remember that they too can. It is better to teach a man to fish than to always show up on his doorstep and hand him a fish every day. Families and friends who experience this growth mindset experience greater relationship success and happiness than people who are always stuck in the same unhealthy and fixed relational dynamics.

Through the above examples, we can see how you can use your growth mindset for social impact. Now, let's dive into exploring how you can create a growth mindset legacy.

Leaving Your Growth Mindset Legacy

It's easy to associate the term "leaving behind a legacy" with historical books and movies that speak about heroes who conquered mighty obstacles. Have you ever thought about "you" leaving a legacy? If yes, what sort of legacy have you always wanted to leave behind in your family or career? If not, why? What made the idea of leaving behind a legacy seem like something you couldn't do?

Many people tend to underestimate how great they are. They become oblivious to the numerous opportunities for leaving lasting legacies that are always present. Why do I say "always"? Because we "always" have problems. If you see these problems as reasons why you can't leave behind a worthwhile legacy, then that is evidence of having a fixed mindset. However, we both know that having a fixed mindset is no longer your cup of tea. This means that the idea of leaving a wonderful and powerful legacy in your family line and career should start to be a familiar pursuit for you now.

But what does it mean to leave a legacy behind, particularly "a growth mindset legacy?" As you may have already guessed, it means being able to create a chain of events or milestones where you choose to be the person who sees problems and adversity as an opportunity to try new things and turn what seemed to be bad into something good. It's being able to stand up and stop hiding behind the crowd. To dare to fearlessly express yourself and pursue success even though checked by failures and frightful risks. It's being the person who refuses to say, "I can't" and says, "We can learn how to do this." It's being able to see beyond your current limitations and help people discover new and better ways to do things. Think about it: How was the airplane even discovered or invented? The Wright brothers imagined a time when they could fly to any place across the world. They believed in what they couldn't see and dared to challenge what people were presently accustomed to by standing up for the vision of the airplane that they conceived. They didn't only let their ideas stay locked up in their heads, but they took action and tried new things until they figured out a way to successfully create the first airplane. Over time, better models of airplanes have been invented. But they will forever be remembered for their legacy of ushering in one of the best inventions of all time: making an airplane. They saw a problem and turned that problem into an opportunity to grow for humanity. This is how their legacy was made in 1903 (History, 2009).

Let's review some of the benefits of leaving a growth mindset legacy:

☞ **It helps you discover and find yourself**: We can never know who we are and what we are capable of unless we embrace challenges and take a leap of faith. Maybe you just limited your abilities to be able to do what you are doing in your job now. But what if there is so much more you can do? If you dare to try something new, apply for that better position, or do something that no one else is courageous enough to do, your legacy starts to grow. You find who you truly are by valuing growth.

☞ **It inspires you to keep opening new doors and making the most of the opportunities around you**: When you start winning battles that you never thought you could, it inspires you to always have a positive attitude toward new opportunities that arise in the future. Instead of shunning them, you are likely to take them on and do your best to overcome them.

☞ **It inspires others to change and do better**: We love reading the stories of all the people who left their legacies, like Mother Theresa, Mahatma Gandhi, Nelson Mandela, and so on. Or maybe in your family you already know some people who are stars. People who dare to challenge their limitations and achieve a better life for themselves—having these role models inspires others to also reach out for a better life. When you leave behind your legacy, it encourages others to change themselves and become better. You inspire generations of people who will also come after you.

☞ **You stop feeling boxed in and stagnant in your life**: Have you ever battled with constantly feeling stagnant and like your life is not improving? All that ends when you start creating your legacy. You begin to manage your time more effectively and actively grow.

☞ **Your mental health starts to flourish**: When we feel stuck, it can mess up our mental health. No one wants to feel like a failure in life. If you purposefully make up your mind to start creating your legacy, all the negative feelings associated with a lack of progress start to disappear.

☞ **Your needs for significance, esteem, and self-actualization are met**: As human beings, we are inherently born with the need to be important, respected, and unleash our best potential. Achieving your growth mindset legacy helps you begin to meet all those needs.

☞ **It helps you build a higher-quality life**: There is no way your life will remain the same if you actively pursue creating a worthwhile legacy. Your relationships, health, career, and overall well-being are likely to elevate. You start to achieve a higher-quality lifestyle.

☞ **It helps you meet and build meaningful relationships**: The less value we have to offer this world, the less people will be interested in us. Building a growth mindset allows you to cross paths with people who also think big, like you would have started to. It helps you connect with people who can propel you forward even more. As people commonly say, birds of the same feathers most usually flock together. You start to repel people who aren't growing and attract those who are serious about progress.

☞ **It increases your self-esteem and self-confidence**: When you look back and see all the things you achieved in your legacy, it naturally boosts your confidence and self-esteem. You no longer see yourself as an incapable and insignificant person. But as a powerful and brave warrior capable of achieving anything you set your mind to.

☞ **Your resilience and self-efficacy grow**: Since most of your victories would have been won amid adversity, it makes you more resilient to problems in life. Instead of running away from them, you start having self-trust and believing in your ability to conquer them if only you try.

Steps to Build a Legacy

1. **Life-examination**: At this stage, you have to take some time to evaluate your life. How much growth do you think you are experiencing in all aspects of

your life? Have you managed to create a meaningful and fun social life over the last few years? Have you managed to climb up your career ladder because of your better contributions at work? Have you managed to improve the quality of your life by trying new things? What's holding you back? What's keeping you playing safe?

2. **What's your unique, powerful strength?** Everyone who achieved a meaningful legacy had something special and unique about them. Some people have refined soft skills, while others are good at particular services. What's your competitive edge? Your gift or talent is what will unlock your breakthrough and legacy.

3. **Be willing to discover and learn about your purpose**: Everything designed has a unique reason why it was made. Likewise, we too can only be fulfilled when we find our true calling and fully apply ourselves to pursuing it and refining our ability to do very well in that area.

4. **Use your legacy to serve your community and celebrate it together with them**: No matter how much success you attain, you can never fully enjoy it unless you have someone to share it with. As much as you want others to celebrate your accomplishments, start also celebrating the efforts others are making in their lives. Share your legacies and uplift your tribe.

How to Establish a Legacy at Work

1. **Start being intentional about taking risks**: You won't always feel like trying out new things. Your current position may feel safe and predictable. However, unless you take new risks, there is no way you can ever create a legacy.

2. **Make lifelong learning one of your core values**: Someone who is always learning can never be stuck in the same place for years. They grow. They may start their career as employees, but because they always learn and improve themselves, eventually, they gain the skills to start their ventures. They become owners of new businesses. Let this become your story by ferociously making learning one of your top priorities.

3. **Your wisdom matters; express it to others**: People can only know how valuable you are to them if you present yourself well. You have to share your wisdom and show others what you are capable of. It's only when people know what you can bring to the table that they will be able to connect you to relevant opportunities and also help you grow.

4. **Start branding yourself**: What do you want to be known for? When we think about certain brands, we either associate them with good-quality products or terrible services. Likewise, you are also a brand. What sort of brand do you want to be known for? Am I an integral, brave warrior who is

always willing to take on new challenges? An effective and efficient co-worker who delivers results in the most organized way possible? What's your brand? Decide on it, and stick to it.

5. **No more small dreams—make room for big dreams and strategically plan how you will achieve them**: We spoke about the power of goal-setting in the previous chapter. Use that information to start making big dreams and big plans for making them happen. New, great ideas can only come if your mind is already thinking about great things. Small dreams beget small thinking. Enlist the help of mentors and others who have already achieved some of the dreams you have, and learn from what worked for them.

The more you apply the growth mindset, your identity starts to grow, and your values become more grounded. You stop settling for less because all your past victories will remind you how powerful you are. Having a growth mindset encourages you to take worthwhile risks when needed. You start to help others grow. When your input in the lives of others makes them better, it benefits you too. Life success is hidden in knowing how to add value to other people's lives. The more you learn how to solve problems, the more legacies you will be able to leave. Hence, moving forward, always look at the challenges in your life as a chance to give birth to the greater version of you. Without adversity, there can never be any legacy to talk about. When you have that paradigm shift, you start to fall in love with growth and be positive about life, no matter what comes your way. It's all meant to work for your good if you let it!

Interactive Exercise

To get you started with putting this knowledge into action, consider doing this simple yet very helpful exercise:

1. List all the problems you are facing in your personal, student, or professional life.

2. Brainstorm possible solutions to those problems.

3. Find out the resources you will need to tackle those challenges.

4. List all the possible good things that can come from turning those problems into opportunities for creating a legacy.

5. What's the worst that could happen if you take the risk of trying new things?

6. Make short- and long-term goals for the problems you will challenge and use as a springboard for your next achievements.

7. Be an accountability partner and ask for advice on how you can turn what's happening in your life into an opportunity for growth and experiencing breakthroughs.

8. Celebrate your progress every step of the way. Remember, it's not about getting everything right; it's about learning every day! That alone means you are already starting to leave behind a legacy.

I'm sure just by reading this chapter; you are so inspired to envision how much your life can transform going forward. Imagine all the unlived dreams waiting for you to just make up your mind to pursue them relentlessly. Imagine how beautiful and fulfilling your relationships, social life, career, and overall quality of life will be when you decide to embrace learning and take action. Now it's time to take full responsibility for the life you want to live and actively start to build it. Nothing can stop someone with a growth mindset!

Conclusion

A growth mindset embraces the belief that your abilities aren't limited but can grow with effort. Self-awareness is needed before anyone can be ready to change. Cultivating a love for learning and a positive mindset when challenges come your way empowers you to be resilient. Through mindfulness and effective goal-setting, your vision for a greater version of yourself can be realized.

When you've lived for a very long time with a fixed mindset, the prospect of embracing a growth mindset can sometimes feel scary and even unattainable. When you feel that way, remember that your old way of thinking is fueling that fear. To break free from that old way of thinking, you have to actively rewire your mind now actively. You can do this by *taking action* towards it. Meaning that despite what you feel, you still practice everything you have learned so far. Everything will change in less than a month of consistently applying these growth mindset secrets. Including you! This is when you will start enjoying the ride even more. Be patient and compassionate with yourself, and always remember to celebrate every new thing you learn.

I am delighted to have read this book. I can't wait to hear about your success story. Please do share it, and feel free to leave a review on Amazon for the book. Now, it's time for you to rewrite your life vision and actively build your growth mindset legacy. If others could do it, surely you can do it too! Let's make it happen together. Sending much love.

Chapter "Good Will"

If so, then here is my small request from you again.

If you've found value in your reading or listening experience today, I humbly ask that you take a brief moment right now to leave an honest review of this book. It won't cost you anything but 30 seconds of your time—just a few seconds to share your thoughts with others.

Your voice can go a long way in helping someone else find the same inspiration and knowledge that you have.

Are you familiar with leaving a review for an Audible, Kindle, or e-reader book? If so, it's simple:

If you're on **Audible**: just hit the three dots in the top right of your device, click rate & review, then leave a few sentences about the book along with your star rating.

If you're reading on **Kindle** or an e-reader, simply scroll to the last page of the book and swipe up—the review should prompt from there.

If you're on a **Paperback** or any other physical format of this book, you can find the book page on Amazon (or wherever you bought this) and leave your review right there.

Thank you so much for your support. You have more power than you realize.

About the Author

Chrío Zoë is a passionate personal development guru. She has written several books on helping people escape their comfort zones and unleash greater versions of themselves. She believes that everyone should have the mind to ferociously pursue and achieve better versions of themselves. True freedom lies in permitting yourself to fly. She hopes that this book will inspire you to unclip your wings and start flying to the greater altitudes that you are meant to be at.

This author has a knack for capturing the essence of life's complexities, intricacies, and universal truths through her writing, often presenting thought-provoking perspectives on various aspects of existence. Her life books are characterized by rich character development, as the author skillfully weaves together the stories of diverse topics, illuminating journeys, challenges, and triumphs. Through books, the author explores themes such as love, passion, victory, identity, personal growth, and the search for meaning, offering readers profound insights and moments of introspection.

Beyond Zoë's professional accomplishments, she also has a rich and multifaceted life outside of publishing. This book is a testament to her commitment to providing valuable insights and practical guidance. The author's books are often praised for their ability to evoke empathy in readers, fostering a deep connection between the readers and the valuable insights they encounter within the pages.

This author is a distinguished authority in various fields of study, bringing a wealth of knowledge and experience to her thought-provoking non-fiction works. As you delve into Zoë's manuscripts, you can expect to embark on an intellectual journey guided by Zoë's profound insights and intentional thought-provoking passion for self -development.   Her non-fiction works continue to push the boundaries of knowledge, inviting readers to expand their horizons and gain a deeper understanding of life and its impact on our success.

Zoë's works have been praised for their meticulous research, insightful analysis, and the way they challenge readers to think critically about the world around them.

Any one of Zoë's latest books....

1. Unlocking Infinity: Master the Art of Longevity
Learn How to, Boost Your Brain Health, Recharge Your Immune System and Restore Youthful Balance in 3 Easy Steps

2. Living Your Best Life: Radiate from Within
Ultimate Guide to Finding Purpose & Fulfillment in 3 Easy Steps.

3. Redefining Aging: The Art of Living Alone
How to Find Joy in Independence, Live Fearlessly & Maintain Longevity

4. Longevity: The Art of Aging Backwards
Step-by-Step Guide to Renew, Restore and Reverse Aging Mentally, Physically & Spiritually

5. Journeying Alone, Journeying Strong: Navigating Aging Alone Without Children
Self-Help Guide to Finding Inner Strength, Peace, Joy & Fulfillment in Childless Aging

6. Alone, But Not Lonely: Aging on Your Terms
A Roadmap for Aging Independently, Striking Balance & Finding Purpose

7. The Positivity Code: Supercharge Your Life with Positive Thinking
Learn The Art of Positive Thinking, Changing Your Life One Thought at a Time

8. Mastering the Steps to Success: Achieving Success at Every Rung
Proven Strategies for Overcoming Obstacles and Reaching Greatness. Develop, Learn, Succeed

9. Superfood Prescription: Refuel Your Mind & Body
100 Supercharged Foods to Revitalize & Transform Your Health

... is another testament to her dedication to delivering enlightening and captivating non-fiction literature. Whether you're a seasoned reader of non-fiction or new to the genre Zoë's work is sure to engage, inform, and inspire.

To stay updated on **Zoë Publishing's** latest projects and musings, visit us on **facebook.com/zoepublishing** and follow us on Instagram & Tik Tok (**@zoepublishing**)

Boureston, K. (2020, January 31). *97 Best unique hobbies – activities to challenge yourself.* Mantelligence. https://www.mantelligence.com/unique-hobbies/

Beres, D. (2016, May 11). *Why mindset is critical in successful relationships.* Big Think. https://bigthink.com/culture-religion/why-mindset-is-critical-in-successful-relationships/#:~:text=

Berns-Zare, I. (2020, February 4). *6 Powerful ways to build new habits.* Psychology Today South Africa. https://www.psychologytoday.com/za/blog/flourish-and-thrive/202002/6-powerful-ways-build-new-habits

Brassey, J., van Dam, N., & Coates, K. (2019, February 19). *Seven essential elements of a lifelong-learning mind-set.* McKinsey & Company. https://www.mckinsey.com/capabilities/people-and-organizational-performance/our-insights/seven-essential-elements-of-a-lifelong-learning-mind-set

Cairns-Lee, Jordan, H., & Jennifer. (2022, August 19). *Escape the shackles of a fixed mindset to unleash growth.* IMD. https://www.imd.org/research-

knowledge/leadership/articles/escape-the-
shackles-of-a-fixed-mindset-to-unleash-growth/

Tools you can use: Finding opportunity in challenge. (2015,
March 17) Change Elemental.
https://changeelemental.org/resources/tools-
finding-opportunity-in-challenge/

Cherry, K. (2022, October 6). *10 Ways to Improve Your
Resilience.* Verywell Mind.
https://www.verywellmind.com/ways-to-become-
more-resilient-2795063

Cherry, K. (2023, July 22). *Self Efficacy: Why believing in
yourself matters.* Verywell Mind.
https://www.verywellmind.com/what-is-self-
efficacy-2795954

What is mindful eating? (2022, January 31) Cleveland
Clinic. https://health.clevelandclinic.org/mindful-
eating/#

Cox, B. (2021, November 2). *Why are challenges important
in life?* Living by Example.
https://www.livingbyexample.org/why-are-
challenges

Davis, T. (2019, April 11). *15 Ways to build a growth
Mindset.* Psychology Today.
https://www.psychologytoday.com/za/blog/click-
here-happiness/201904/15-ways-build-growth-
mindset

DePaul, K. (2021, February 2). *What does It really take to
build a new habit?* Harvard Business Review.

https://hbr.org/2021/02/what-does-it-really-take-to-build-a-new-habit

Fairbanks, B. (2021, August 4). *10 helpful habits to develop a lifelong learning mindset | Tips and activities.* University of Phoenix. https://www.phoenix.edu/blog/develop-lifelong-learning-mindset.html

Goals and Planning. (2020, August 13). *7 Examples of how successful people set goals and achieve them.* Stunning Motivation. https://stunningmotivation.com/how-successful-people-set-goals/

Greenhalgh, N. (2023, September 5). *How to move from a fixed mindset to a growth mindset.* Daniels College of Business. https://daniels.du.edu/blog/how-to-move-from-a-fixed-mindset-to-a-growth-mindset/

Hall, E. D. (2017, March 31). *Mindful Listening | Psychology Today South Africa.* https://www.psychologytoday.com/za/blog/conscious-communication/201703/mindful-listening

Ho, L. (2020, March 10). *9 Inspiring growth mindset examples to apply in your life.* Lifehack. https://www.lifehack.org/865689/growth-mindset-examples

Hughes, G. (2020, March 20). *Fixed mindset and growth mindset: How to Evolve Your Mind For Ultimate Success.* Age of Awareness.

https://medium.com/age-of-awareness/fixed-mindset-and-growth-mindset-how-to-evolve-your-mind-for-ultimate-success-983b6f95f7f9

Jacob. (2022, February 7). *Why Is challenge important in life (And The 5 Best Challenges!).* You Can Fly Mate! https://youcanflymate.org/why-is-challenge-important-in-life/

JD. (n.d.). *Best Motivational Short Stories About Personal Growth, Mindset, and Productivity.* Sources of Insight. https://sourcesofinsight.com/best-motivational-short-stories/

jon18a. (2019, October 31). *The science behind mindset - within health.* Create Health Marketing. https://createhealth.com/2019/10/31/the-science-behind-mindset/

Joseph, S. (2016, November 5). *How to see challenges as opportunities.* Psychology Today South Africa. https://www.psychologytoday.com/za/blog/what-doesnt-kill-us/201611/how-to-see-challenges-as-opportunities

Katz, L. (2020, May 6). *How do we grow through challenges?* Psychology Today. https://www.psychologytoday.com/us/blog/here-we-are/202005/how-do-we-grow-through-challenges#

Leslie, I. (2014, July 31). *Seven ways to be more curious.* Psychology Today South Africa. https://www.psychologytoday.com/za/blog/findin

g-the-next-einstein/201407/seven-ways-be-more-
curious

Linder, J. N. (2021, March 11). *4 ways mindfulness traits and practices build resilience*. Psychology Today South Africa.
https://www.psychologytoday.com/za/blog/mindf
ulness-insights/202103/4-ways-mindfulness-
traits-and-practices-build-resilience

Llopis, G. (2014, February 20). *5 Ways a legacy-driven mindset will define your leadership*. Forbes.
https://www.forbes.com/sites/glennllopis/2014/02
/20/5-ways-a-legacy-driven-mindset-will-define-
your-leadership/?sh=38a2727616b1

Mathers, C. (2020, February 26). *27 Habits to develop the growth mindset in your Life*. Develop Good Habits.
https://www.developgoodhabits.com/growth-
mindset/

MD, A. E. B. (2021, May 13). *Can mindfulness change your brain?* Harvard Health.
https://www.health.harvard.edu/blog/can-
mindfulness-change-your-brain-202105132455#

Kickstarting *a growth mindset in yourself and those you manage*. (2019, April 2). Media Partners.
https://www.mediapartners.com/blog/post/kickst
arting a growth mindset in yourself and those
you manage

Meisner, C. (2020, July 16). *How having A growth mindset can change your life.* Blog.mindsetworks.com. https://blog.mindsetworks.com/entry/how-having-a-growth-mindset-can-change-your-life

Mindsetworks. (2015). *What's my mindset?* Blog.mindsetworks.com. https://blog.mindsetworks.com/what-s-my-mindset

Moore, C. (2019, May 27). *How to set and achieve life goals the right way.* PositivePsychology.com. https://positivepsychology.com/life-worth-living-setting-life-goals/

Newman, K. M. (2017). *How to be a lifelong learner.* Greater Good. https://greatergood.berkeley.edu/article/item/how_to_be_a_lifelong_learner

Nortje, A. (2020, June 5). *How to practice mindfulness: 10 Practical steps and tips.* PositivePsychology.com. https://positivepsychology.com/how-to-practice-mindfulness/

Perry, E. (2023, August 2). *Leaving a legacy: What It means and how to leave one (+ Examples).* Betterup. https://www.betterup.com/blog/leaving-a-legacy#

Ph.D, N. C. (2020, August 15). *What is Mindful Breathing? Exercises, Scripts and Videos.* PositivePsychology.com. https://positivepsychology.com/mindful-breathing/#

Robson, D. (2020, March 13). *How a "growth mindset" can lead to success.* BBC. https://www.bbc.com/worklife/article/20200306-the-surprising-truth-about-finding-your-passion-at-work

School of Education. (2020, December 10). *How to foster a growth mindset in the classroom.* American University. https://soeonline.american.edu/blog/growth-mindset-in-the-classroom/

Spector, C. (2019, September 30). *"Embrace the struggle": Stanford education professor challenges common beliefs about teaching and learning.* Stanford. https://news.stanford.edu/press-releases/2019/09/30/embrace-struggleeaching-learning/#:~:text=September%2030%2C%202019-

Suarez Angelino, L. (2022, July 6). *The 54321 method: benefits & how to use it.* Choosing Therapy. https://www.choosingtherapy.com/54321-method/

The many benefits of lifelong learning. (n.d) Walden University. https://www.waldenu.edu/programs/resource/the-many-benefits-of-lifelong-learning#